ADVENTURERS OF OREGON

TEXTBOOK EDITION

∴

THE CHRONICLES
OF AMERICA SERIES
ALLEN JOHNSON
EDITOR

GERHARD R. LOMER
CHARLES W. JEFFERYS
ASSISTANT EDITORS

LEWIS AND CLARK ON THE COLUMBIA RIVER

From the painting by Frederic Remington

ADVENTURERS OF OREGON

A CHRONICLE
OF THE FUR TRADE
BY CONSTANCE L. SKINNER

NEW HAVEN: YALE UNIVERSITY PRESS
TORONTO: GLASGOW, BROOK & CO.
LONDON: HUMPHREY MILFORD
OXFORD UNIVERSITY PRESS

1921

CONTENTS

ILLUSTRATIONS

ADVENTURERS OF OREGON

.·.

CHAPTER I

THE RIVER OF THE WEST

HISTORIC Oregon emerges from myth. Over the region of those "continuous woods" which shrouded the true River of the West, the romancings of ancient mariners had spread the mirage of a great inland waterway called the Strait of Anian. This waterway threaded the continent from sea to sea, among wondrous isles gorgeous with palaces, and linked Europe to Asia. Into the Strait of Anian, so the legend ran — and gathered magic as it ran — flowed a mighty river, the River of the West. This river had its source in the Mountains of Bright Stones, in the heart of the continent, and its broad equable tide was well adapted to bear fleets of treasure ships into the strait that made so convenient a short cut between Spain and the sublime East.

1

The first Adventurers of Oregon were therefore certain Latin and Levantine seamen, who, for the glory of some king, said that they had bravely sailed and even meticulously charted these strange waters of their own fancy! Truly, in their tales, as Bancroft says, "maritime lying reaches the climax and borders on the heroic." There was no Strait of Anian such as they described.[1] Yet where the imagination of these romancers coursed among fabulous isles, one lucky American seaman, after three centuries of naval fantasy, discovered the Columbia River flowing scarf-like over the shoulder blade of the continent. And it was chiefly by virtue of that discovery that the wilderness empire of Oregon found its destiny within the United States of America.

But we may not leave the myth of the direct passage to Asia with merely a passing reference; it has had too potent an influence upon history for such casual treatment. It dates back to Columbus, of course. Columbus discovered America; but he

---

[1] The documents relating to these early myths are printed in the first volume of Bancroft's *History of the Northwest Coast.* The name of one of the romancers is perpetuated in the name of the strait discovered in 1787 by Barkley, an English trader, and named by him in honor of Juan de Fuca, a Greek pilot, whose gallant ship was said to have breasted Anian's waters in 1592.

did not discover that pathway to the Orient which
he was seeking, nor that the round world was much
larger and Asia much smaller than he had calcu-
lated them to be. He died believing that somewhere not far behind the new lands he had found
lay the Asiatic coast, and that somewhere — to the
south, he thought — opened a direct sea passage
whereby the galleons of Spain might the swifter
reach and bear homeward "the wealth of Ormus
and of Ind."

The mystery of the short route to Asia concerned
Spain very particularly. Spain was the leading
maritime nation of the world, with Portugal a
close second; but now that all Europe was agog for
discovery, how long would it be before other nations — France, or perhaps even England — should
challenge her rights? How should Spain guard
against the encroachments of other nations with
oversea ambitions? In some such manner reasoned, with disquiet minds, their Spanish majesties
who had financed Christopher's voyages. They
appealed to the Pope to define the boundaries of
Spanish possession. So Alexander VI, generous
and of helpful intent, drew a line through the
Atlantic from pole to pole, and gave all that lay
west of the line to Spain and all that lay east of it to

Portugal. Surely not even the lore of Olympus, where high gods made merry with a world of little men, offers a scene so rich and quaint as that which we may conjure up from the story of Pope Alexander dividing the world between his children, as if it were but a rosy apple. Their Spanish majesties feared, indeed, even after such fair apportionment, that it might yet prove to be an apple of discord. They resolved therefore to have the western passage discovered without delay, secretly if possible, and fortified at both entrances.

Thus began the great search which inspired most of the explorers in the New World during three centuries. The Cabots, Balboa, Magellan, Cortés, Cartier, De Soto, Drake, Hudson, La Salle, were adventurers who set out to make a reality of the great discoverer's dream. Not all of them were Spaniards; and thereby was it proved that Spain had not groundlessly doubted whether the Pope's award would long satisfy those nations which had received no portion of it!

The first mariner actually to sail north of the southern boundary of the present State of Oregon is supposed to have been the Spanish seaman after whom Cape Ferrelo is named. Ferrelo set out in

1543 from Panama where the Spaniards had planted their first colony on the Pacific. He appears,
however, to have left no record of having landed.
Perhaps the northern waters, in his estimation,
promised little; at any rate his voyage led to no
further northward explorations at that time. The
Spanish interests of that day lay in the south; and
it was indeed a golden south, where Spanish seamen loaded their ships with wealth wrung from the
enslaved and terrorized natives and then sailed
homeward to spread the hoard at the King's feet.

It was the loss of some of these treasure ships, or
rather of their contents, in 1579 — a loss occasioned by the unwelcome activities of a certain
Francis Drake from England — that once again
turned Spanish sails northward in a search for
the hidden passage. Not only had Drake swooped
down as a conqueror upon waters and shores belonging exclusively to Spain, not only had he escaped to England with loot from Spanish vessels,
but he had discovered the desired passage and
had sailed through it — so the Spaniards believed.
Drake, of course, had not discovered the passage,
though he had gone northward for that purpose,
desiring some other homeward route than the one
frequented by Spanish ships. He had, however,

anchored in Oregon waters and had taken possession, for his Queen, of the long rolling coast to the south, naming it New Albion — prophetically naming it so, for although Spain was to be overlord of this coast for centuries, it was to pass finally into the hands of a people speaking their law in the English tongue.

The fearsome tales told thereafter of the red-bearded English corsair miraculously steering his treasure-crammed ship, the *Golden Hind* — the very name sounded supernatural — into the mysterious passage, inspired Spanish seamen to seek that passage anew; for by what way the terrible Drake, "laughing athwart the decks," had gone he might even again return.

But if Drake thus, in a legendary rôle, inspired the mariners of Spain to new search for the hidden passage, he presently, in his proper person, put a curb on Spain's activities and humbled her pride upon the sea. And for two hundred years after those ten days in July, 1588, when Drake scattered the blazoned sails of the Armada upon the rocks and tide-rips of the North Sea, Spain had little heart for maritime exploration in any quarter of the globe. Had it not been for that achievement of Elizabeth's seamen far from Pacific shores, who knows what might have happened on the west coast of America north of Mexico? Or on the east coast? With Spain mistress of the seas, could Englishmen have obtained a foothold on either coast to drive a continental wedge between the Spanish on the south and the French on the north? The defeat of the Armada, remote as it seems, in fact decided that the laws and language of England should prevail in America.

Two centuries passed. Once again Spanish seamen of the south turned north to seek the western gate of that hidden passage. It was shortly after the accession of Carlos III to the Spanish throne, in 1759, that Spain's ambition for world power, which had been somnolent since the disaster of the Armada, awoke once more. Drake's countrymen meanwhile had settled along the Atlantic seaboard, which coast also Spain held to be hers *de jure*, if not *de facto*. Thus had the English spread already to the New World their religious heresy and their peculiar ideas of government. In the very year when Carlos ascended the throne, they had broken the blade of France on the heights of Quebec; and in one year more they had practically swept from the northeastern parts of America that autocratic system of government and those social ideals which were the fundaments of Spanish power, no less than of French.

When Carlos of Spain was ready to give his attention to the northern half of the New World, the English colonists — either ignorant of or indifferent to the Spanish decree that, whatever truce Spain might hold with England in Europe, there should be "no peace beyond the line" — were already beginning their thrust westward towards the heart of the continent. Moreover, Spain's domination of the Pacific coast was seriously threatened by another power from the north. Russian fur hunters had overrun Siberia to the shore of the Pacific, where they had established headquarters at Kamchatka. In 1741 Vitus Bering, a Dane sailing for the Russian Czar, had discovered the Aleutian Isles and the strait that bears his name. And now the Russians were masters of Alaska, reaping enormous wealth from their yearly harvest of sea otter and seal. Now, therefore, more than ever was it vital to Spain that the hidden channel should be discovered, its banks fortified, and its waters closed forever to all but Spanish keels.

So, in 1774, the Spanish Viceroy of Mexico dispatched Juan Perez to make a thorough exploration of the Northwest Coast. The time seemed auspicious for New Spain. True, the English had swept away the French and in this very year were battling with the Indians beyond the Appalachians for the rich territory of the Ohio; and far to the north the traders of the Hudson's Bay Company were pushing westward. But the storm of revolution was gathering in the American colonies. If the winds but continued to blow advantageously for Spanish statecraft, the passing of that storm should see Spain arbiter of the whole New World. The acquirement of Louisiana from France, in 1763, signified Spanish intent to press in from the south and west upon the English colonies. And, to forestall Russia, the interloper in Alaska, the whole of the Northwest Coast must be explored and formally annexed to New Spain.

From Bruno Heceta, who followed Perez's route and made a landing in 1775 at the present Point Grenville to establish Spanish claims, comes the first mention that is not legendary of the River of the West. Heceta did not discover a river, but he noted in his journal that, when anchored near the forty-sixth parallel, his observations of the currents had convinced him "that a great quantity of water rushed from this bay on the ebb of the tide." Illness among his crew as well as other mishaps prevented Heceta from entering to explore the bay where the River of the West — still unseen of white men — emptied its foaming and roaring waters.

By 1776 the Northwest Coast had been thoroughly explored, so Spanish mariners reported, as far north at least as Sitka, although neither the Strait of Anian nor the River of the West had been discovered. Spain, however, made no move to occupy the land, as there seemed no immediate danger from Russia, and the American Revolution, as Spanish and French statesmen saw it, was ultimately to bring the revolting colonists into the fold of their Latin allies. In pursuance of the usual Spanish policy of secretiveness, Spain did not publish any account of the explorations of her seamen. But in 1778 a Yankee named Jonathan Carver published in London a book purporting to be a record of his travels across the American continent, in which he related as fact what Indians had told him of the great River of the West rising among the Mountains of Bright Stones and flowing into the Strait of Anian. The name of this great river, said Carver, was the Oregon; and a map proved the tale. This book contained some truth, for apparently Carver did penetrate beyond the Mississippi, but it contained also not a little myth and

a great deal of padding from untrustworthy sources.
Today the one important bit in the book is the grand
name "Oregon."   Is it an Indian word, or a word
of Spanish derivation, or did Carver invent it?   No
one knows.   It seems not to have been used again
until 1811 when William Cullen Bryant retrieved
it and immortalized it in *Thanatopsis:*

> . . . Take the wings
> Of morning, pierce the Barcan wilderness,
> Or lose thyself in the continuous woods
> Where rolls the Oregon, and hears no sound
> Save his own dashings. . . .

Two years before the appearance of Carver's
book, that is, in 1776, when England and her
American colonies were locked in bitter strife, the
British Admiralty had sent Captain Cook to explore the Northwest Coast of America.   One of the
aims of this expedition, of course, was the discovery
of the passage; for the officers and crew of any
ship of His Majesty's discovering that passage
would receive twenty thousand pounds sterling,
an award offered by Parliament in 1745 and still
standing.   Cook anchored off Nootka, Vancouver
Island, on March 29, 1778, and then sailed north
until forced by ice to turn back.   He wrote in his
journal: "Whatever passage there may be, or at

least part of it, must lie to the north of latitude
72°," which was indeed so. The only actual passage was the impracticable northern strait already
discovered by Bering. Cook then crossed to the
Asiatic coast and thence to the Sandwich Islands,
where he was killed by natives. His voyage to
the Northwest Coast had results. It was made the
basis of England's claims in the quarrel with Spain
about Nootka ten years later. More important,
however, was the introduction of Englishmen to
the sea-otter trade. A few sea-otter skins had
been presented by the natives at Nootka to Cook
and his men; and when Cook's ship arrived at
Canton, after the tragedy at the Sandwich Islands,
these furs were bid for by Chinese tradesmen at
what seemed to the English seamen fabulous sums.

Trade! Furs convertible into gold! Here was
the potent influence to bring out of the realm of
myth the land "where rolls the Oregon." Since
the days when Elizabeth had answered Philip of
Spain out of the mouths of Drake's guns, England
had consistently refused to concur in Spain's doc-
trine that the Pacific was a closed sea. So when
the news of furs on the Pacific coast of America
was bruited about English ports, English merchants lost no time in preparing expeditions for

trade with the natives of that far country. As for the direct passage, let the explorers look for it; as to the Spanish fiat, let the diplomats wrangle about it. Honest merchants were neither to be lured by an invisible channel nor barred by an intangible principle from new paths of trade. Presently four separate fur trading expeditions — one from China, two from India, and one from England — ploughed Pacific waters.

One of these, sailing from Bengal, was commanded by John Meares, late of the British navy. Though Meares made Nootka his headquarters, he, too, like Cook, had some influence on Oregon. He was an enterprising soul and a brisk trader, hardly more scrupulous than other men of his class at that time. Since he was obliged to sail along a so-called Spanish coast, he hoisted the Portuguese flag when convenient, and perhaps left it flying at the *Felice's* masthead while he went ashore at Nootka and purchased the place — with boundaries unspecified — from Chief Maquinna for some copper and a pair of pistols, and denoted it not Portuguese but British soil. He erected buildings of a primitive sort and "occupied." He shipped some Chinese workmen from their native land, gathered up Kanaka wives for them at Hawaii —

possibly with the idea that the less conversation
between married folk the more harmony — and
proceeded to colonize Nootka. He was well received by the Indians. His description of the welcome given him is worthy of reproduction, for
the sake of the picture it gives us of the chiefs
Maquinna (or Maquilla) and Callicum and their
warriors, a scene the like of which can never recur.
Meares wrote in his journal, on May 16, 1788:

They moved with great parade about the ship, singing
at the same time a song of a pleasing though sonorous
melody: there were twelve of these canoes, each of
which contained about eighteen men, the greater part
of whom were cloathed in dresses of the most beautiful
skins of the sea otter, which covered them from their
neck to their ancles. Their hair was powdered with
the white down of birds, and their faces bedaubed with
red and black ochre, in the form of a shark's jaw, and
a kind of spiral line which rendered their appearance
extremely savage. In most of these boats there were
eight rowers on a side. . . . The Chief occupied a
place in the middle, and was also distinguished by an
high cap, pointed at the crown, and ornamented at the
top with a small tuft of feathers. We listened to their
song with an equal degree of surprise and pleasure. It
was, indeed, impossible for any ear susceptible of de-
light from musical sounds, or any mind that was not
insensible to the power of melody, to remain unmoved
by this solemn, unexpected concert. . . . Sometimes

they would make a sudden transition from the high to the low tones, with such melancholy turns in their variations, that we could not reconcile to ourselves the manner in which they acquired or contrived this more than untaught melody of nature. . . . Everyone beat time with undeviating regularity, against the gunwale of the boat, with their paddles; and at the end of every verse or stanza, they pointed with extended arms to the North and the South, gradually sinking their voices in such a solemn manner as to produce an effect not often attained by the orchestras in our quarter of the globe.

After the concert, the chiefs brought aboard the *Felice* a skin bottle of seal oil, in which exhilarating beverage Meares and his guests pledged their eternal friendship.

Having thus established amicable relations with the Indians, Meares set about erecting buildings and a fort, and he also built a little ship, the *North-West America*, the first vessel to be constructed on the Northwest Coast. He explored southward in search of Bruno Heceta's river, or the River of the West. He did not find it, though he crossed the bar and stood near enough to its mouth to name the spit of land hiding it Cape Disappointment, and the harbor beyond, Deception Bay.

His colony soon came to grief. The year 1789 saw two other expeditions in these waters. One hailed from the Spanish port of San Blas, Mexico, and the other from Boston. The Viceroy of Mexico had bethought him that it was now three years since he had sent up the coast a sea scout to report what the Russians were doing. Spain had graciously permitted the Russians to occupy Alaska, but with the distinct proviso that their ramshackle trading craft were not to nose southward. It was high time to ascertain if this understanding were perfect on both sides. The Viceroy therefore sent north Don Estevan Martinez, captain of the *Princessa*, which was no trading vessel but an imposing ship of war bristling with guns. Martinez made some startling discoveries. He learned that the Russians were about to push down to Nootka; he found at Nootka the Meares colony; he found also riding at anchor in Nootka Sound, besides an English vessel, the *Iphigenia*, two other vessels flying the Stars and Stripes, the *Columbia*, Captain John Kendrick, and the *Lady Washington*, Captain Robert Gray, both of Boston. Meares himself was absent on a voyage to China. Martinez seized the colony and the English vessels, the *Argonaut*, the *Princess Royal*, and the *North-West America*, as they sailed into port, quite unaware of the Spanish intruder. He took Captain Colnett of the *Argonaut* a prisoner to Mexico. He did not molest the American vessels.

England promptly demanded redress for the seizures at Nootka. Spain answered haughtily, rattled the sword, and made a gesture to her cousin of France, who nodded agreeably and took down the family armor and began polishing it publicly. But the earth beneath the Bourbon's palace at Versailles was already quivering from the subterranean rumblings of the French Revolution, and Spain saw that the aid she had counted upon was uncertain at best. Spain was obliged therefore to sign articles which, besides reimbursing the enterprising Meares for his losses, restored Nootka to the British flag, and acknowledged the right of British subjects to free and uninterrupted navigation, commerce, and fishing in the North Pacific; also to make and possess establishments on the Pacific coast wherever these should not conflict with the prior rights of Spain. Though the articles defined the rights of only the contracting parties, England and Spain, yet in signing them Spain abrogated her ancient claim to sole sovereignty on the Pacific; and, whether either party realized it or not, in this document both concurred

2

in the principles of a free sea and of ownership by occupation and development.

But those Americans, Kendrick and Gray, trading at Nootka under the Stars and Stripes — who were they? Of them history tells not so much as we would like to know. They were in the service of a group of merchant adventurers in Boston, friends of Doctor Thomas Bulfinch of Bowdoin Square. These merchants, we are told, on a winter evening in 1787, forgathered in the Doctor's library and, fired by a published account of Cook's voyages, then and there decided to enter the sea-otter trade in the Pacific. Joseph Barrell, a prosperous trader and banker, seems to have taken the lead in the enterprise, in which Bulfinch himself joined. The other partners were Crowell Hatch, Samuel Brown, John Pintard, and John Derby. These were gentlemen traders of the old school, and theirs was the happy lot to live in the heyday of Boston's adventuring upon the sea, when four hundred sail might often be counted in the harbor by any worthy merchant, such as Joseph Barrell, as he loitered on his way to the Bunch of Grapes, the famous old tavern on the site of the present Exchange. It was at the Bunch of

Grapes that the Boston Marine Association held its meetings.

The partners procured and made ready for sea a ship, the *Columbia*, and a little sloop, the *Lady Washington*. The vessels were stocked with trinkets to trade with the natives for furs. The voyage was to be a long one, around the Horn, around the whole world, indeed, for the *Columbia* would sail from the Pacific coast to China, there exchange a cargo of furs for a cargo of tea and silk, and return home to Boston. It was the 1st of October before all was ready for the voyage. Then, after the usual celebrations on board, the *Columbia*, under command of John Kendrick, and the *Lady Washington*, under command of Robert Gray, lifted anchor and put out to sea, and the partners went back to their daily round to await the return of the *Columbia* with a rich cargo from China.

Nearly three years rolled by. Then, one day in August, 1790, into Boston harbor sailed Robert Gray on the *Columbia*. He and Kendrick had spent two seasons gathering furs on the coast; there they had found the British trader Meares and had seen his post raided by the Spaniard Don Martinez; they had exchanged ships in the Pacific, where Kendrick remained to continue the trade.

Gray had taken the furs to Canton and now brought home a cargo of tea. The furs had not sold well in Canton; perhaps Gray was not a good trader; at all events, the results in trade were disappointing. But, for the moment, the partners forgot their losses. Had not their own ship, the *Columbia*, circumnavigated the globe? All Boston turned out in its best attire to welcome Gray as he marched up the street followed by his Hawaiian attendant in a bright feathered cloak; and Governor John Hancock held a reception in his honor.

The partners met once more in Bulfinch's library. Two of them decided to withdraw, but the others considered the prospects promising enough to warrant a second venture. So the good ship *Columbia* was overhauled and made ready for sea again.

On September 28, 1790, Robert Gray sailed out of Boston harbor on his second voyage around the Horn. On June 5, 1791, he arrived at Clayoquot, the American trading post on Vancouver Island. That summer the Yankee adventurers fared not too well. Gray sailed as far north as Portland channel, where some of his men were murdered by hostile Indians. His comrade in adventure, Kendrick of the *Lady Washington*, also met with tragedy. The natives of Queen Charlotte Island attacked Kendrick's ship and his men on shore; and his son was among the slain. The two ships returned to Clayoquot in September and Kendrick set out for China with the furs. Gray erected at Clayoquot a fort and constructed a little sloop, named the *Adventure*, which he put under command of Haswell, his second officer. The Indians about Clayoquot were not friendly, and during the winter Gray and his men were obliged to exercise constant watchfulness to avert a meditated attack. On April 2, 1792, both vessels left Clayoquot, the *Adventure* turning north for trade and the *Columbia* dropping southward. Perhaps Gray was only bent on finding new trading fields, for sea otter were still plentiful to the south of Vancouver Island. Yet his movements suggest that he may have been consciously exploring, searching for that passage which was supposed to lie somewhere hidden, or for the River of the West.

It was in October, 1790, the month following the *Columbia's* departure from Boston, that England and Spain signed the articles relative to Nootka and to mutual rights on the Pacific. In December George Vancouver, a British naval officer, who had sailed with Cook as a midshipman, received his commission to go to Nootka to take over from Spanish emissaries the land seized by Martinez and to explore. Vancouver's ships left Falmouth, England, on April 1, 1791. They rounded the Cape of Good Hope, crossed the Indian Ocean, and sailed along the western coast of Australia, made Van Diemen's Land, New Zealand, the Society Islands, and the Sandwich Islands, whence they set sail for the Northwest Coast of America. They sighted that coast in 39° north latitude on April 17, 1792. At dawn on the twenty-ninth of the same month, as they headed northward, the English mariners descried a sail, the first they had seen in many months of wandering over the watery wilderness. The stranger ship declared herself by firing a gun and sending the American colors to the masthead. The *Discovery*, under Vancouver's personal command, hove to for an exchange of greetings and news. The American vessel was the *Columbia*, and her commander, Captain Robert Gray, informed Vancouver that he had recently lain for nine days off the mouth of a large river where the reflux was so violent that he dared not attempt to enter. Gray had also sailed for many miles through the narrow waters of the Strait of Juan de Fuca and was now

heading south again, to make a second attempt to
enter the river which lay behind the forbidding,
foam-dashed wall of Cape Disappointment.

Despite the information given him by the American, Vancouver believed that he could not have
passed any "safe navigable opening." He had indeed noted in his journal, in passing Cape Disappointment, that he had not considered "this opening worthy of further attention." Gray's news
impressed him therefore but slightly. He jotted
down in regard to it: "If any river should be
found, it must be a very intricate one and inacces-
sible to vessels of our burden." He pushed on
northward. He discovered and explored Puget
Sound, naming it after one of his lieutenants. He
named Mount Baker in honor of another lieutenant who was the first man on board to descry that
white crown of beauty. He explored the mainland
of British Columbia and, circumnavigating the island that now bears his own name, swung down
to Nootka where the Spanish Commissioner, Don
Quadra, awaited him.

But of far greater moment was the feat which
Robert Gray, the Yankee seaman and fur trader,
had in the meantime accomplished. Gray had

run his ship past the spur of Cape Disappointment
and into the mouth of the great river.   This is the
entry he made in his log, May 7, 1792:

Being within six miles of the land, saw an entrance
in the same, which had a very good appearance of a
harbor. . . .   We soon saw from our masthead a
passage in between the sand-bars.   At half past three,
bore away, and ran in north-east by east, having from
four to eight fathoms, sandy bottom; and, as we drew
in nearer between the bars, had from ten to thirteen
fathoms, having a very strong tide of ebb to stem. . . .
At five P.M. came to in five fathoms water, sandy
bottom, in a safe harbor, well sheltered from the sea
by long sand-bars and spits.

Within the harbor the *Columbia* was speedily surrounded by Indians in canoes, and trading continued briskly for several days.   The canoes having departed, the *Columbia* "hove up the anchor,
and came to sail and a-beating down the harbor."
By the 11th of May, Gray was ready to attempt
the entrance of the river itself.   This is how he
narrates that historic event:

At eight A.M. being a little to windward of the entrance of the Harbor, bore away, and run in east-
north-east between the breakers, having from five to
seven fathoms of water.   When we were over the bar,
we found this to be a large river of fresh water, up

which we steered. At one P.M. came to with the small bower, in ten fathoms, black and white sand. The entrance between the bars bore west-south-west, distant ten miles; the north side of the river a half mile distant from the ship; the south side of the same two and a half miles' distance; a village on the north side of the river west by north, distant three-quarters of a mile. Vast numbers of natives came alongside; people employed in pumping the salt water out of our water-casks, in order to fill with fresh, while the ship floated in. So ends.

Not an imaginative man, this Robert Gray, and no stylist. He had found the great River of the West. He had made fact of the myth beloved of the ancient mariners. And he sets down his discovery laconically as if it were no more than an incident of a trading voyage — just one brief matter-of-fact paragraph and *So ends!* It is almost, indeed, as if he considered the discovery of this river, which he named the *Columbia,* unimportant. Other sea wanderers had sought it; some of them had even fancifully charted it, so great had been their faith. Explorers, dreaming of vast inland seas and golden rivers, of jeweled cities to be discovered and of colonies to be founded — some of them scientific men, too — seeking this river had passed it by.

But, if Robert Gray was no writer, we may nevertheless, from his terse jottings, read the character of a man too literal-minded to suspect other men of the gift for artistic fable — a matter-of-fact man who reasoned that, if Bruno Heceta had felt the current made by a river, then the river which made the current was there — and, more, a man of plain courage, an experienced sailor with an impartial estimate of his own seamanship and with a mind not to be appealed to by the things that touch imaginative men with fear; one who saw merely winds to beat against and tides to gage and make use of, where other men saw a Cape Disappointment looming over the grave of ships.

Gray sold his furs in China and returned to Boston in 1793. The results must have fallen below expectations, for he was not sent out again. Kendrick of the *Lady Washington* was killed in Hawaii by a gun explosion. Gray's discovery apparently impressed the public little more than it had impressed Gray himself, for it was not followed up in any way for some years. Neither recognition nor wealth was bestowed upon the discoverer. Gray died in 1806 at Charleston, and he died in poverty.

CHAPTER II

LEWIS AND CLARK

THOUGH Gray suffered eclipse, and though the Government of the United States maintained an attitude of indifference towards his discovery, there was one American statesman with that vision of his nation's natural domain which had inspired the sweeping phrase "from sea to sea" in the charters granted to the first English colonists. Thomas Jefferson dreamed of expansion to the Pacific Ocean for at least twenty years before the way opened to put his desire into effect. In December, 1783, he had written on this matter to George Rogers Clark, whose military genius during the Revolution had given the young Republic its farthest western boundary. The fact that the British at this time entertained the idea of exploration overland apparently had its influence on Jefferson, for he wrote:

I find they have subscribed a very large sum of money in England for exploring the country from the

Mississippi to California. They pretend it is only to promote knowledge. I am afraid they have thoughts of colonising into that quarter. Some of us have been talking here in a feeble way of making the attempt to search that country. But I doubt whether we have enough of that kind of spirit to raise the money. How would you like to lead such a party? tho I am afraid our prospect is not worth asking the question.

Jefferson's doubts as to the prospects were evidently justified, for nothing was done. Three years later in Paris, as American Minister, Jefferson listened sympathetically to a young countryman named John Ledyard, who had sailed with Cook and who was eager to cross the continent from the North Pacific. His plan included the establishment of trading posts and the exploration of the intervening unknown territory for the purpose of laying claim to it in the name of his country. Jefferson gave Ledyard the only assistance in his power, which was to request the Empress of Russia to permit Ledyard to cross her domains. She refused, but nevertheless the young explorer set out to traverse Siberia to Kamchatka, whence he was to go by sea to Nootka, and essay the crossing of the continent. In Siberia he was arrested by the Russian authorities, who were aware of his plans with regard to the fur trade, and was carried back to Poland. He made his way to France and presently joined an exploring expedition bound for Africa. There he perished.

The American chronicles of these years are all but silent on the theme of Pacific exploration. In 1793, the year after Gray's discovery of the River of the West, Jefferson made a positive effort to set an expedition on the way to the Pacific by land. Again, as in 1783, apparently he did not find "enough of that kind of spirit to raise the money" among the elect of Congress, for it was the American Philosophical Society which responded to his plea. A French botanist named André Michaux was chosen to make the journey in the interests of science. If the selection of Michaux satisfied the American Philosophical Society, it did not at all please a certain Virginian youth who was one of Jefferson's friends. This youth, who was just finishing his education at a Latin school, was more than willing to forgo further literary wanderings in the company of Virgil's hero for the sake of writing in action an epic of his own on the virgin soil of the West. But Meriwether Lewis, at eighteen years of age, failed to convince the philosophers or Jefferson that he possessed the qualifications and experience requisite to make a success of the

venture. The wise men might better have entrusted their affair to this valiant American boy
than to the Frenchman Michaux, for no sooner
had the botanist reached Kentucky than his scientific mind revolted from the peaceful study of sta-
mens and pistils and exercised itself busily with
military intrigue.

Another decade elapsed without further progress, though the passing years were not without
their events and their lessons. Spain conceded to
Americans the right of navigation on the Mississippi; but, before the concession, the secret machinations of Spanish agents had kept the trans-
Appalachian commonwealths in perpetual ferment.
The diplomacy of Spain in respect to Kentucky
and Tennessee, however, served the purpose of
arousing the American authorities to the danger
threatening the young Republic — the danger of
being hemmed in on three sides by hostile powers
and thus barred from expansion. In 1800 Spain
secretly ceded Louisiana to France, stipulating that
the territory should not be ceded to any other
power without Spain's consent. The transfer became known to American statesmen and increased
their uneasiness. On the north, in Canada, were
the none too friendly British; to the south were

the Spanish; and now Louisiana, with its vast and
undefined boundaries, had come into the possession
of France — the militaristic France of Napoleon
Bonaparte. And, in 1802, Napoleon was planning
a military and colonizing expedition to New Orleans
to strangle the commerce of the United States on the
Mississippi and to occupy his new colonial empire
lying between that river and the Rocky Mountains.

Meanwhile, in March, 1801, Jefferson had become President of the United States. He made
two attempts to purchase from France and Spain
New Orleans and the Floridas. His failure in both
instances no doubt had not a little to do with the
determination he reached in January, 1803, to send
an expedition to the Pacific coast — to the mouth
of that River of the West discovered in 1792 by
Robert Gray. Because the expedition must proceed as far as the Rockies across country which
lay within the vague boundaries of Louisiana and
which therefore was foreign soil, its true character
and intents must be kept secret. So Jefferson, in
the private message sent by him to Congress,
asked for an appropriation of $2500 for a "literary
pursuit."

While other civilized nations have encountered great
expense to enlarge the boundaries of knowledge by

undertaking voyages of discovery, and for other literary purposes, in various parts and directions, our nation seems to owe to the same object, as well as to its own interests, to explore this the only line of easy communication across the continent, and so directly traversing our own part of it. The interests of commerce place the principal object within the constitutional powers and care of Congress, and that it should incidentally advance the geographical knowledge of our own continent can not but be an additional gratification. The nation claiming the territory, regarding this as a literary pursuit, which it is in the habit of permitting within its dominions, would not be disposed to view it with jealousy. . . . The appropriation of $2500 "for the purpose of extending the external commerce of the United States," while understood and considered by the Executive as giving the legislative sanction, would cover the undertaking from notice and prevent the obstructions which interested individuals might otherwise previously prepare in its way.

While Jefferson's expedition was in preparation in the spring of 1803, it happened that Napoleon experienced a change of heart in regard to Louisiana because the Mistress of the Seas was clearing her decks for war on him. Napoleon was now anxious to get rid not of New Orleans alone but of the whole territory. Whatever motives may have contributed to his swift decision, he took satisfaction in the belief that he had given England a rival that should one day humble her pride. That no spirit of good-will towards the United States inspired him is evident from his remark that the Louisiana territory "shall one day cost dearer to those who oblige me to strip myself of it, than to those to whom I wish to deliver it."

In fact, Napoleon believed that he was selling to the United States, at a stiff price, a Pandora's Box of troubles. Some of his malign prophecies had a temporary fulfillment. In biblical language, which narrates evils as transient experiences, they "came to pass" — came and passed. And we may wonder today what thoughts would have agitated the mind of Napoleon if he could have seen the fleets of England and America keeping guard together in the North Sea while, on the soil of France, Britons from five lands fought side by side with Americans and Frenchmen for France; or could he have looked upon an American people unified from coast to coast and from the Rio Grande to the Canadian line, with little else than a yearly Mardi Gras Carnival at New Orleans to remind them that the Louisiana territory, forming now the greater part of thirteen States, was once in the possession of a hostile France and was sold to America with a curse.

3

Jefferson paid for Louisiana $15,000,000. The treaty of purchase was signed in May, the month of England's declaration of war, and ratified by the Senate in October, 1803. It will be seen that Napoleon did not allow the conditions of his treaty with Spain to stand in his way. Spain, however, could do nothing but suffer indignantly. Jefferson's expedition to the mouth of the Columbia would make its way westward across all American territory. The Fates seemed propitious for the enterprise.

Having won the coöperation of Congress, Jefferson's next move was to select a leader. His choice fell upon that same young Virginian who, ten years before, had advanced his claim against that of the unstable French botanist. Meriwether Lewis since then had gone far to qualify himself for the great adventure. He had become a captain in the regular army and had taken a gallant part in the frontier wars; and, as Jefferson's private secretary since 1801, he had convinced the President of his fitness to lead the expedition. In Jefferson's *Memoir* we find the following:

I had now had opportunities of knowing him intimately. Of courage undaunted; possessing a firmness and perseverance of purpose which nothing but impossibilities could divert from its direction; careful as a

father of those committed to his charge, yet steady in
the maintenance of order and discipline; intimate with
the Indian character, customs, and principles; habitu-
ated to the hunting life; guarded, by exact observation
of the vegetables and animals of his own country,
against losing time in the description of objects already possessed; honest, disinterested, liberal, of sound
understanding, and a fidelity to truth so scrupulous
that whatever he should report would be as certain as
if seen by ourselves — with all these qualifications, as
if selected and implanted by nature in one body for this
express purpose, I could have no hesitation in confiding
the enterprise to him.

Portraits of Lewis confirm Jefferson's description.
They show a finely formed head and a face elo-
quent of courage, of integrity, and intelligence.

Lewis took up the desired task with energy.
Conscious of his need of astronomy and natural
science in order to make faithful geographical
notes, he spent some time in Philadelphia "under
tutorage of the distinguished professors of that
place." He personally supervised the construction of the necessary boats and arms; and he wrote
to his friend, William Clark, inviting him to join in
the splendid adventure and offering him equality
with himself in command and honors. William
Clark, then with his brother, George Rogers Clark,
at Clarksville, Tennessee, where Lewis desired him

to enlist frontiersmen for the expedition, accepted the invitation with a light-heartedness equal to his friend's. It is this enthusiasm, bubbling frequently into mirth, which makes Lewis and Clark's journals — even when the journals record days of peril and severe hardship — such live reading.

William Clark, born in Virginia in 1770, was four years older than Lewis. He had joined his brother, George Rogers, in Louisville at the age of fourteen and had fought in the Indian wars, first under his brother and later under Charles Scott and "Mad Anthony" Wayne. He was described in 1791 as "a youth of solid and promising parts, and as brave as Cæsar." He was a tall man, strongly built, with bright red hair and blue eyes; his brow was broad, his not handsome features were strongly marked, and the expression of his countenance was friendly and firm. As a young officer under Wayne he had acquitted himself with a dignity and an adroitness beyond his years on important missions to the Spanish authorities in Louisiana. But he was no scholar, as the original spelling in his journal shows.

The personnel of the expedition included forty-three men besides the two leaders. The men, nearly all of them young, were enlisted from among the

Kentucky frontiersmen and from the western garrisons. Among the Kentucky volunteers were sons, or other kin, of the men who had first crossed the Appalachians with Daniel Boone and who had held Kentucky through the bloody Indian raids of the Revolution and won the Illinois country under the leadership of George Rogers Clark. Some of the regular army men, indeed, were taken from the Kaskaskia garrison. One of the young frontiersmen was Charles Floyd, a kinsman of that John Floyd who fought in Dunmore's War, the war which pushed the white man's frontier from the Appalachians to the Ohio River — in the year 1774, the year of Meriwether Lewis's birth. The guide was a Frenchman named Charboneau, who brought with him his Indian wife Sacajawea, the Bird-Woman. Clark's servant York, a huge black man, accompanied his master. The three boats specially built to convey the expedition up the Missouri River were two pirogues and a bateau fifty-five feet long, which was propelled by a sail and twenty-two oars and boasted a forecastle and cabin. Besides arms and munitions, the bales in the boats contained presents for the Indians, mathematical instruments, medicines, meal, and pork, and a variety of camp equipment.

The explorers wintered at the mouth of the Wood River opposite the mouth of the Missouri, waiting till spring should dissolve the ice, breaking the routine of their camp by frequent hunting trips. On May 14, 1804, to quote Clark, having crossed the Mississippi, they "proceeded on under a Jentle brease up the Missourie." The speed of their boats, under favorable conditions, was from twelve to fifteen miles a day. On the afternoon of the sixteenth, Clark with the boats reached St. Charles, twenty-five miles up the stream, and here Lewis, who had been detained at St. Louis, joined him on the twentieth. They set out the next day, making slow progress because of shifting sand bars and crumbling cliffs. Once, at least, a falling bank almost swamped one of the pirogues and the men had to jump overboard and hold the boat steady until the current swept away the sand.

After four days of such travel they reached La Charette, a tiny village and the last outpost of civilization. Here Daniel Boone was living at this time, filling the office of syndic, or magistrate; and here the explorers hove to for the night, pitching camp just above the village. On the next day they said farewell to the last white habitation they were to see until their return two years later and pushed on into the unknown.

Their troubles with sand bars, snags, and falling banks continued, but they met those troubles gaily. Frequently they stopped for hunting, for forty-five lusty explorers could consume a goodly quantity of fresh meat. They were not yet quite alone in the wilderness, for sometimes they met the descending pirogues of trappers and hunters who were bringing their winter's harvest of furs and deerskins to St. Louis. From one of these parties they engaged an interpreter named Dorion to facilitate their intercourse with the Siouan tribes through whose territory they would pass.

By the middle of June, mosquitoes and flies were upon them in clouds. In places the driftwood and snags were so thick that they must chop their way through them. Their oars were already worn out and they were obliged to cut timber and shape new ones. On the twenty-sixth they reached the mouth of the Kansas River, having traveled some three hundred and forty miles from their starting point at the mouth of the Missouri. Where Kansas City stands now, Lewis and Clark found the lower villages of the Kaw or Kansas Indians, a tribe "not verry noumerous at this time," owing to wars. An important part of Lewis's duties, in accordance with Jefferson's instructions, was to establish trade relations with the Indians along the route and to make them understand that the territory wherein they dwelt was now a part of the United States whose President was the Indians' Great Father. In the interests of science, as well as of commerce, Lewis was also to learn whatever he could of Indian habits and languages and to note the differences and similarities between the various tribes. His copious notes in *A Statistical View of the Indian Nations Inhabiting the Territory of Louisiana* furnish us, indeed, with the only information we have concerning some of the tribes of that time as they were before contact with the white race had changed them.

The Fourth of July was celebrated near the site of the present Atchison, Kansas, by firing a salute and by a dance. There was a fiddler among the men and he and his fiddle did their tuneful service on all occasions when there was a fête day to honor or when a succession of hardships had tinged the crew's mood with glumness. Throughout the whole march, when the shadow of defeat crept down, it was banished by a round of grog and the sound of the fiddle calling on the men to dance.

And they danced. Sometimes hungry, sometimes sure that the dangers already experienced had led them only into an impasse where they were about to perish, often sore-footed and spent, they danced — and all was well again. On this first Independence Day in the wilderness the captains not only ordered a salute and a dance, but they had a christening as well. They named two creeks Fourth-of-July and Independence. The latter still ripples under the name given it by its godfathers, Lewis and Clark, perhaps the first white men to spy its waters.

On the 3d of August Lewis held council with chiefs of the Otoes, a branch of the Pawnees, on a cliff about twenty miles above the present city of Omaha. This cliff Lewis and Clark named the Council Bluff. Lewis was the chief spokesman at the council, while Clark "Mad up a Small preasent for those people in perpotion to their Consiquence." Speeches were made by the chiefs in answer to Lewis's "talk," and gifts were exchanged. With buffalo robes and painted skin tents the chiefs responded to the medals and gold-braided uniforms bestowed upon them. Here Liberté, a Frenchman, deserted and, although searched for, was not to be found; but a soldier, Reed, who attempted the same thing was recaptured and punished by being made to run the gauntlet several times while being soundly beaten with rods. Lewis and Clark, in keeping with the ideas of their time, believed in severe penalties. Their journals record one other instance of insubordination — in which the culprit received seventy-five lashes on his bare back. Perhaps it is not surprising that there were so few incidents of the sort to set down.

Sometimes Lewis recorded the day's events; sometimes Clark was the diarist. Not only by the orthography (Clark spelled as he listed and capitalized adjectives or prepositions as the humor seized him) is it easy to trace each author. Lewis pictures Nature's handiwork with a touch of romance as well as with a carefulness of detail which shows that the instruction he received from the "distinguished professors" in Philadelphia has not been wasted. Clark's entries reveal the keen observation of the frontiersmen. His accuracy is a natural gift, trained solely by woodsman's experience and for practical purposes. A gorgeous sky does not leave him cold, but his first thought about it is concerned with its prophecy of weather. As for instance when he notes that "at Sunset the atmespier presented every appearance of wind,

Blue & White Streeks centiring at the Sun as She disappeared and the Clouds Situated to the S. W. Guilded in the most butifull manner." The "appearance of wind" was a matter of very practical import to the expedition which was being pushed up the stream by sail as well as by oars. It had its bearing on the safety of the night camp, and on the chances of the hunt. Generally in the same spirit, Clark notes rapids and bluffs and the outlines of banks and the quality of soils. A bad stretch of portage compels him to cast an appraising eye over the river falls which cause his discomfort. He is interested, too, in setting down the personal incidents and gossip of each day. So that in reading his entries we get illuminating sidelights on the characters and dispositions of the men as well as of their leaders. Clark's narrative, realistic and "human," runs side by side with Lewis's — with its scientific data, its flashes of wit, and its romantic enthusiasms — and supplements it in a way that makes the Lewis and Clark *Journals* a unique literary work and a perfect example of collaboration.

On the 20th of August, Clark records the only death which took place on the journey. Charles Floyd "Died with a great deel of composure. . . .

a butifull evening." Today a tall obelisk on
Floyd's Bluff, Sioux City, Iowa, marks the grave
of the first American who fell in that country in
the cause of civilization.

As they neared the mouth of the Big Sioux
River, the explorers heard from Dorion, the interpreter, an interesting story. Near the source of
that river, he said, there was a creek which flowed
in from the east between high cliffs of red rock. Of
this red stone the Indians made their pipes. And,
since pipes were a supreme necessity in both their
domestic and political life, they had established a
law under which that region was held sacred to
peace. Tribes at war with each other met there
to mine the brilliant stone, without the least show
of hostility, and there an Indian fleeing from his
foes might find sure refuge. Among these jagged
red cliffs the fugitive was as one "between the
horns of the altar."

On the twenty-third, Fields, one of the party,
had the honor of killing their first buffalo; and, a
week or so later, Lewis shot an antelope and intro-
duced the prairie dog to science. The journal here
has a long account of the Dakota Sioux, with whom
Lewis and Clark held councils. One of these councils threatened to turn out badly. Clark went

on shore "with a view of reconsiling those men
to us." The Indians seized a pirogue and were
"very insolent both in words and justures" so
that Clark drew his sword and made a signal to
the boat to prepare for action. The Indians who
surrounded him drew their arrows from their quiv-
ers and were bending their bows, when the swivel
in the boat was instantly pointed toward them,
and "those with me also Showed a Disposition
to Defend themselves and me. I felt My Self
warm & Spoke in very positive terms." The Sioux
chief, impressed by this resolute front, ordered the
warriors to draw back. Clark continues, "after
remaining in this Situation Sometime I offered my
hand to the 1. & 2. Chiefs who refused to receive
it." Presently the chiefs changed their minds,
however, as Clark turned away towards the boats.
They waded in after him and he invited them on
board. So, through a frank show of both warlike
courage and good-will a peril was passed. The conclusion of Clark's story of the event discloses that
strain of buoyancy in both leaders which must have
been one of the strongest bonds of their friendship.
After proceeding about a mile they anchored off a
little island overgrown with willows which they called
"bad humered Island as we were in a bad humer."

They had now been for some weeks in the big game country. Deer, buffalo, elk, antelopes, wolves, and bears were seen frequently in herds and packs. On the 19th of October they saw fifty-two herds of buffalo and three herds of elk. Two days later they passed the Heart River a little below the spot where a railway bridge now joins the towns of Bismarck and Mandan. Advance gusts from oncoming winter assailed the explorers as they hastened on, passing nine ruined villages of the Mandans in whose chief towns they intended to make their winter camp. They reached their destination on the twenty-sixth; and in the first week of the following month they began the building of their fort, on the east bank of the Missouri, about twenty miles beyond the present town of Washburn, North Dakota. They had traveled some sixteen hundred miles from their starting point.

A relict of the Mandan tribe lives today on the Fort Berthold reservation, but there are very few full-bloods among them. In 1804 the Mandans numbered over twelve hundred. They were sufficiently unlike the other plains tribes to cause much romantic speculation as to their origin. They were fairer skinned; and light hair was not uncommon among them. They wore their hair very long, sometimes trailing to their heels. They lived in earthen houses, well built, circular in shape with slightly domed roofs. They were cultivators of the soil, with no lust for warfare; and consequently they were despised and raided by the ferocious Sioux. It was their boast, then and afterwards, that they had never shed the blood of a white man. Lewis and Clark were not the first white men they had entertained. The Canadian explorer La Vérendrye spent a part of December, 1738, with them. They were familiar with the traders of the North-West Company and of the Hudson's Bay Company. Some of these traders, indeed, came to the Mandan villages while Lewis and Clark were wintering there.

Buffalo hunts were among the diversions and duties of the winter months. Lewis had ample time to study the Mandans and to inscribe their legends and history as well as to collect and prepare specimens of various sorts to send to President Jefferson in the spring. To give a practical proof of the American Government's friendship for its Mandan children, Clark offered to go out with a number of the men of the expedition and a party of Indians to pursue and punish a band of Sioux who had attacked some Mandans. The Indians were greatly pleased at this compliment; but, as the snow was thick and the going bad, they preferred to take the will for the deed. In February the exploring party was augmented by one papoose, a boy, his mother being Sacajawea, the young Indian wife of Toussaint Charboneau the guide.

On April 7, 1805, the explorers left Fort Mandan and pushed on up the Missouri in canoes and pirogues. The more imposing bateau was now headed down stream, manned by thirteen men who vowed to bring it safely to St. Louis. Its precious contents included, besides specimens, skins, Indian articles, buffalo robes, and other trophies for Jefferson, a report from Lewis and a copy of Clark's diary. The spirit which animated not only the leaders but the rank and file is attested to by Lewis in his letter to the President. Of the men who were to guide the bateau, Lewis wrote: "I have but little doubt but they will be fired on by the Sioux; but they have pledged themselves to us that they will not yeald while there is a man of them living."

Lewis and Clark's party now numbered thirty-two persons. Following the list of their names we read that Charboneau and his wife, with her infant, accompanied the expedition as "Interpreter and interpretress." Sacajawea was a Shoshone who had been captured when a child by Minnetarees and by them sold as a slave to Charboneau. The old *voyageur* brought her up and afterwards married her. From now on we are to find the young Indian woman, Sacajawea, gradually taking a prominent part in the councils of the expedition.

On the 26th of April the explorers passed the mouth of the Yellowstone River and gave it its English name, translated from the French *rochejaune*. Three days later Lewis had a lively encounter with two "brown or yellow bears" of a sort new to him. One of these animals, wounded by Lewis, pursued him for "seventy or eighty yards" but only to its own death, for Lewis managed to reload and kill it — and so made the scientific discovery of the grizzly bear. From now on "yellow" bears, "white" bears, and "brown" bears, all variously tinted grizzlies, appeared with disturbing frequency, and whenever they caught sight of an explorer they gave chase. One brown-furred guardian of the wild, with seven bullets in him, forced the intruding hunters to throw down their guns and pouches and leap twenty feet into the river; he plunged in after his foes and had all but snapped upon the hindmost when a shot from

4

the shore put the eighth ball in him and ended the
chase. This happened on the 14th of May. It
was surely a day of tests for the explorers. While
the hunters were fleeing from Bruin, a squall struck
a canoe under sail and upset it, with the assistance of Charboneau, who completely lost his head:
"Charbono cannot swim and is perhaps the most
timid waterman in the world." Fortunately the
little vessel, which contained "our papers, instruments, books, medicine . . . and in short almost every article indispensibly necessary to further the views, or insure the success of the enter-
prize in which we are now launched to the distance
of 2200 miles" was not completely overturned. But
the lighter articles were washed overboard and
were saved only by the cool courage and nimble
fingers of Charboneau's wife, the Bird-Woman,
who snatched back most of them from the hungry
stream. In this merry fashion did the explorers
celebrate the anniversary of their setting out from
the mouth of the Wood River.

The Missouri now wound about the base of tall
cliffs of white sandstone sculptured by wind and
water into grotesque shapes. Perhaps it was this
remarkable environment that stirred the practical Clark into a romantic mood and led him to

christen a stream they passed presently, "Judith's River," in honor of the lady of his heart whom he afterwards married. Clark was one of those to whom a rose by any other name would smell as sweet; the lady's name was, in fact, Julia Hancock, not Judith. Nevertheless the Judith River still marks the map of Montana in her memory. A little later Lewis also complimented a lady, his cousin Maria Wood, though the turbulent waters of Maria's River (now written Marias) "but illy comport with the pure celestial virtues and amiable qualifications of that lovely fair one."

At Maria's River, on the 2d of June, they came to a halt, for they did not know which of the two streams was the Missouri. Here the party divided. Lewis with six men set off to investigate Maria's River, and Clark proceeded up the south fork, the Missouri. Both leaders had serious encounters with grizzly bears, besides other difficulties, before they returned to the forks; but they returned of one mind, convinced that the south fork was the Missouri. What manner of leaders they were is revealed in the fact that their party willingly turned up the south fork with them, although all the men were also of one mind, but in the opposite conviction.

Leaving Clark in charge of the boats, Lewis proceeded up the river on foot, until he heard a distant rush of waters and saw spray rise above the plain like a column of smoke and immediately vanish. The noise, increasing as he approached, soon "began to make a roaring too tremendious for any cause short of the great falls of the Missouri." Then the Falls came into view. Lewis hurried down the banks of the river, which were two hundred feet high and "difficult of access," and sat on a rock below the center of the Falls to enjoy "this truly magnificent and sublimely grand object, which has from the commencement of time been concealed from the view of civilized man." The Great Falls were more than a sublime spectacle to Lewis and Clark; they were proof positive that the explorers were on the true Missouri, heading towards the passes that led into the region of the Columbia River.

While waiting for the boats, Lewis explored the surrounding country, and he crowded a great deal of excitement into the few days. He shot a buffalo and was waiting to see it drop when he discovered a brown bear within twenty steps of him. He had forgotten to reload, so that there was nothing for it but flight. The bear, open-mouthed, pursued him, gaining fast. The plain was bare of trees or brush. Lewis decided that his only chance was to plunge into the river and force the bear to attack under the handicap of swimming. His ruse was successful. But a little later, as he continued his explorations, three buffalo bulls ran at him. Lewis writes: "I thought at least to give them some amusement and altered my direction to meet them; when they arrived within a hundred yards they made a halt, took a good view of me and retreated with precipitation." He now pushed rapidly through the dark towards camp to escape from a place which "from the succession of curious adventures" seemed to him an enchanted region. "Sometimes for a moment I thought it might be a dream, but the prickley pears which pierced my feet very severely once in a while . . . convinced me that I was really awake." He made his bed that night under a tree and awoke in the morning to find a large rattlesnake coiled on the trunk just above him.

Clark, with the boats, was meeting dangers of another sort. "We set out at the usual time and proceeded on with great difficulty . . . the current excessively rapid and difficult to assend great numbers of dangerous places, and the fatigue which we have to encounter is increatiatable the men in the water from morning until night hauling the cord & boats walking on sharp rocks and round slippery stones which alternately cut their feet & throw them down, notwith standing all this dificuelty they go with great chearfulness, aded to those dificuelties the rattlesnakes inumerable & require great caution to prevent being bitten." Of the five falls on the Missouri two received from Lewis and Clark the names they still bear — Great Falls and Crooked Falls.

At this point, of course, navigation became impossible. To reach free water again it was necessary to make a portage of about seventeen miles. The men shaped wheels from the one lone cottonwood tree on the bank and made axles and tongues of willow and other light woods within reach. With these they moved the laden canoes across the rough surface of the plain which was dented deep by the hoofs of the buffalo. The hard dried edges of the dents tortured the men's moccasined feet and made hauling difficult and slow. The tongues and axles broke repeatedly and had to be renewed. But the men were helped sometimes by high winds, which blew the canoes under sail at a good pace over the earth. They had stumbled across rough country for thirteen days when at last they reached the launching point above the Falls.   Then, while Cruzatte, the French *voyageur*, scraped his fiddle, all who could make use of their feet had a dance on the green.

On the 29th of June, Clark, Charboneau, and the Bird-Woman and her baby almost lost their lives in a cloud-burst.   They had taken refuge from the rain in a narrow ravine when suddenly a torrent descended upon them.   "The rain appeared to descend in a body and instantly collected in the rivene and came down in a roling torrent with irresistible force driving rocks mud and everything before it which opposed it's passage.   Capt C fortunately discovered it a moment before it reached them and seizing his gun and shot pouch with his left hand with his right he assisted himself up the steep bluff shoving occasionally the Indian woman before him who had her child in her arms; Sharbono had the woman by the hand indeavoring to pull her up the hill but was so much frightened that he remained frequently motionless and but for Capt C both himself and his woman and child must have perished."   The water rose so swiftly that it was up to Clark's waist before he had begun to climb and "he could scarcely ascend faster than it arrose till it had obtained the debth of 15 feet with a current tremendous to behold. One moment longer & it would have swept them into the river just above the cataract of 87 feet where they must have inevitably perished." In this adventure Clark lost his compass, Charboneau dropped his gun, shot pouch, and powder-horn, and the Bird-Woman had barely time to grasp her baby before the net in which it lay at her feet was swept away. Some of the men had been out on the plain when the storm broke and the heavy hail, driven upon them by the violent wind, had felled several of them so that they were "bleeding freely and complained of being much bruised."

The explorers had been for some time, of course, in sight of the Rocky Mountains, and, while not unimpressed by the grandeur and beauty of the great range, they were doubtless thinking more of the passes among the peaks which they must find and penetrate. On the 13th of July, they took stream again at a point about three miles above the present city of Great Falls, Montana; and on the twenty-fifth they reached Three Forks, the confluence of the three rivers which unite their waters to form the Missouri. These rivers were named by Lewis and Clark the Madison, the Jefferson, and the Gallatin.

They were now in the country of the Snakes, or Shoshones, the Bird-Woman's people. Near by Sacajawea pointed out the very spot where she had been captured. Eagerly she watched for signs of her tribe, minutely examining deserted brush wickiups to discern how recently they had been tenanted, straining her eyes for smoke signals among the blue mists on the mountains.

Sacajawea, searching the sunlit horizon or looking wistfully out into the dusk as it drifted down and extinguished her hope of that day, was little understood by the two busy leaders, who had already noted in their journal that, true to the Indian character, she viewed the old scenes with indifference. But her preoccupation provoked her lord and master, so that one evening he dealt her a blow, for which Clark gave him a "severe repremand."

At length, after navigating the shallows and canyons of the Jefferson to a point near the present town of Dillon, Montana, the explorers met with a company of famishing Shoshones, pressing on eastward to the buffalo grounds along the Missouri. Lewis, exploring by land, had found them first and with difficulty had persuaded them to remain to greet the boat party. These Indians were so often the prey of the fierce Blackfeet that they were intensely nervous and suspicious. The appearance of the boats reassured them, and so great was the relief of their frightened chief that he fell upon Lewis's neck and repeatedly embraced him till he was "besmeared with their grease" and "heartily tired of the national hug." The party disembarked. The eager Bird-Woman raced ahead and presently, says Clark, "danced for the joyful sight," as she held out her arms to a young woman who rushed towards her. The two had been companions in childhood and had also been together in captivity.

The Shoshone chief took Lewis and Clark to his lodge. His warriors quickly marked a small circle in the sod, in the center of the tent, by tearing up the bunch grass; and here Indians and white men seated themselves on green boughs covered with antelope skins. Then the sacred pipe was brought. Clark was enough impressed with this pipe to make a drawing of it; and, from his picture and written description, we can see its long stem and its large bowl of green stone, polished like crystal and gleaming like jade, as the chief slowly gestured with it to the four points of the compass. But though the white men knew that the chief meant

them well because he had taken off his moccasins — as one who said, "May I forever go bare-
foot if I deal not truly with you" — yet they
could not make their needs known to him. And
those needs were great. For here, at the foot of
the high Mountains of Bright Stones, all their
hopes would end unless this chief could be influenced to guide them through the pass. They
knew that it would not be easy to persuade him to
part with horses enough for their party and baggage; and, as they regarded his "fierce eyes and lank
jaws grown meagre from the want of food," they
doubted if anything they could offer would induce
him and his starving tribe to turn back from their
hunting trip. So Sacajawea was sent for, not only
to interpret but to plead, as a Shoshone, with her
kin to open the sealed door in that great stone
barrier that the white men might go on to the wide
waters of the River of the West.

It was surely a dramatic moment for the Bird-
Woman when she slipped into the formal council
circle, with head bent and eyes downcast as became
a woman among chiefs. But a keener experience
was in store for her. As the chief began to speak,
telling the white men that not by his war name but
by his peace name, Cameahwait, or Come and

Smoke, would he be known to them, the Bird-
Woman recognized her brother. She sprang up
with a cry, ran to him, and threw her blanket about
him, weeping. The chief also was deeply moved
by this strange meeting, and for a brief moment
the white men caught a glimpse of the universal
human heart beating behind the racial barrier.
"The meeting of those people was really affecting,"
Lewis writes. Lewis and Clark could only guess at
the meaning of Sacajawea's long earnest speech to
her brother, but they could heartily rejoice at its
results, for the chief agreed to fulfill all their desires.

The explorers had now to adapt their outfit to
overland travel; so they set about making pack-
saddles. For nails they used rawhide thongs; and,
for boards, oar handles and the planks of some of
their boxes encased in rawhide. While the crew,
assisted by the Indian men, were at this task, the
Indian women were busy mending the white men's
moccasins. Though the chief had promised that
the Shoshones would help transport the baggage
and see the party safely over the mountains, yet
on the day before the departure he secretly prepared to go down the Missouri to the buffalo
grounds. Taxed with his double-dealing, he admitted it to Lewis regretfully, explaining that the

tribe's food supply had come to an end and that, seeing his people in want, he had forgotten his promise to the white men, which, however, he would now fulfill at all costs. In this incident we get a pure white flash of the young Bird-Woman's character, for, despite her joy in the reunion with her kin, her loyalty to Lewis and Clark moved her to betray to them the change in her brother's plans which so menaced the success of the expedition.

Moved by these experiences among the Shoshones, Lewis, in one of his most thoughtful moods, thus records his birthday, the 18th of August:

This day I completed my thirty-first year, and conceived that I had in all human probability now existed about half the period which I am to remain. . . . I had as yet done but little . . . to further the happiness of the human race, or to advance the information of the succeeding generation. I viewed with regret the many hours I have spent in indolence and now soarly feel the want of that information which those hours would have given me had they been judiciously expended. But since they are past and cannot be recalled, I dash from me the gloomy thought, and resolved, in future, to redouble my exertions and at least indeavour to promote those two primary objects of human existence, by giving them the aid of that portion of talents which nature and fortune have bestoed on me; or in future, to live *for mankind*, as I have heretofore lived *for myself.*

The party crossed the backbone of the Rockies through the Lemhi Pass and entered a wild country of deep gorges, mad streams, and thickly wooded mountain flanks. Here Sacajawea's kinsmen took leave of the white men and returned to the eastern side of the range — all but one old Shoshone who consented to remain and guide the expedition, for the explorers had still to encounter grave perils before the navigable waters of the Columbia River would ease their travel. Clark spent a week in fruitless explorations of the branches of the Lemhi and the Salmon in Idaho. There was no clear river highway here. The expedition then pushed northwest through the hills and, veering east, passed the Continental Divide into Montana again. Here Lewis and Clark had friendly encounters with Nez Percés and Flathead or Salish Indians. On the 7th of September they camped south of the present Grantsdale, Montana. They pressed on northward to Lo Lo Creek, named by them Travelers Rest, and crossed again into Idaho through the Lo Lo Pass. Heading towards the Clearwater, the Shoshone guide sometimes mistook the trail and it seems that the expedition floundered about. The men suffered from hunger, from cold and fatigue. They were obliged to kill a horse occasionally for food. Sometimes the main party halted, while Clark with some of the hunters went out searching for a way out of the maze of foaming streams and snow-crowned precipices. But by the twenty-sixth all were safely camped on the Clearwater. Both leaders and men were very ill from the privations they had undergone; nevertheless they began building canoes at once. On the 7th of October they were headed down the river and three days later they camped near its mouth. Then, launching their canoes on the Snake, they came on the sixteenth to the mouth of that river which pours its waters into the Columbia itself. Here Indians, as though to celebrate the great event — the significance of which they could not have grasped had it been told to them — collected in numbers to receive the white men. "A Chief came from this camp which was about ¼ of a mile up the Columbia river at the head of about 200 men singing and beeting on their drums Stick and keeping time to the musik, they formed a half circle around us and Sung for Some time."

On the 18th of October Lewis and Clark floated out upon the River of the West. They portaged the Celilo Falls on the twenty-third and took stream again in that stretch of the river known as

the Dalles where the water runs over lava beds
and between grotesquely carved lava cliffs. The
navigators presently saw ahead of them a tremendous rock stretching across the river leaving a channel "between two rocks not exceeding *forty five*
yards wide" through which the whole body of the
Columbia must press its way. A portage here
was considered by Clark "impossible with our
Strength"; he therefore "deturmined to pass
through this place notwithstanding the horrid appearance of this agitated gut swelling, boiling &
whorling in every direction, which from the top of
the rock did not appear as bad as when I was in it;
however we passed Safe." Two days later they
passed the Long Narrows, where their canoes were
nearly swamped by the boiling tide, and camped on
Quinett Creek near the present city of The Dalles.
Then one more bad stretch of water, the Cascades,
must be portaged before the ease of continuous
unobstructed navigation was theirs. On the 7th of
November, according to Clark, there was "Great
joy in camp, we are in *view* of the *Ocian*, . . .
this great Pacific Octean which we have been so
long anxious to See, and the roreing or noise made
by the waves brakeing on the rockey shores . . .
may be heard distictly."

It would seem that what they saw, however, was not the ocean but the mouth of the Columbia, which is over a dozen miles wide at this point below the site of the future Astoria. They now experienced the ocean swells which roll through the river here and also the blowing rain and fog characteristic of the Northwest Coast. Their first camp was on Point Ellice, called by Clark Point Distress. Here for several days they were not only drenched to the skin but pelted with stones which the rains loosened from the hillside. In this wretched condition they remained, wet and cold, and with only a little dried fish to satisfy their hunger. The men were scattered on floating logs or trying to shelter themselves in the crevices of the bank. Here also "we found great numbers of flees which we treated with the greatest caution and distance." The weather cleared on the 15th of November and the explorers moved round the point into Baker's Bay, where they built shelters for themselves with the timbers from the walls of an abandoned Indian village. Their journey had occupied eighteen months and had covered four thousand miles. On the rugged wilderness from the mouth of the Missouri to the Pacific Ocean, Lewis and Clark and their loyal band had written America's greatest epic of adventure. Here they were now at the mouth of Robert Gray's river; and presently we see the indefatigable Clark climbing joyously to the top of Meares's Cape Disappointment. On one side of him rolls a free sea; on the other stretches a wooded cliff line which shall be the western shore of the United States.

Lewis and Clark wintered among the Clatsop Indians, south of the Columbia, a few miles up the Lewis and Clark River, where Lewis pursued his ethnological studies and the others passed the time in hunting and exploring.

On March 23, 1806, the expedition turned homewards. On the 30th of June, having recrossed the Great Divide through Lo Lo Pass and reached Travelers Rest Camp, a mile above the mouth of Lo Lo Creek, the leaders decided on the dangerous plan of separating the party to make explorations. On the 1st of July Lewis wrote:

From this place I determined to go with a small party by the most direct rout to the falls of the Missouri, there to leave [three men] to prepare carriages and geer for the purpose of transporting the canoes and baggage over the portage, and myself and six volunteers to ascend Maria's river with a view to explore the country and ascertain whether any branch of that river lies as far north as Lat^d 50. and again return and join the party who are to decend the Missouri, at the entrance of Maria's river . . . the other part of the men are to proceed with Capt Clark to the head of Jefferson's river where we deposited sundry articles and left our canoes. from hence Sergt Ordway with a party of 9 men are to decend the river with the canoes; Capt C with the remaining ten including Charbono and York will proceed to the Yellowstone river at it's nearest approach to the three forks of the Missouri, here he will build a canoe and decend the Yellowstone river with Charbono the indian woman, his servant York and five others to the missouri where should he arrive first he will wait my arrival. Sergt Pryor with two other men are to proceed with the horses by land to the Mandans and thence to the British posts on the Assinniboin [Clark says, "the tradeing Establishments of the N W Co"] . . . to prevail on the Sioux to join us on the Missouri.

In consequence of this daring plan, which was not fully carried out in detail, the party was separated for six weeks. Lewis explored Maria's River and found that it had no branches reaching to the fiftieth parallel. His excursion, however, was not uneventful, for he exchanged shots with the war-like Blackfeet and later was shot accidentally and painfully wounded by Cruzatte, the fiddler, who mistook his leader for a deer. The Bird-Woman accompanied Clark's party. It was she who recognized signs obliterated to other eyes, who pointed

out the true passes in the maze of hills and ravines and guided the party safely to Three Forks.
From Three Forks Clark set out to explore the
Yellowstone River to its mouth. On the journey
he mapped many points now famous, such as the
Big Horn mountains and river, the plain where
Custer's monument now stands, and the huge rock
called Pompey's Pillar on which Clark's signature
and the date cut in with his knife are still legible.
He lost all his horses, which were silently rounded
up and driven away by Crow Indians. Descending the river, near the present city of Glendive,
Clark and his men were forced to halt for an hour
because the river, though a mile wide, was occupied
from shore to shore by the crossing of a buffalo
herd. The next day they witnessed the crossing
of two herds.

One of Clark's companions was John Colter.
This man returned to the Yellowstone River in
1807, and was, so far as is known, the first white
explorer of the mountains of Wyoming between the
Big Horn Range and the Idaho border. He discovered the Three Tetons and Yellowstone Lake
and some part at least of Yellowstone Park.

By the 14th of August Lewis and Clark were
once more among the Mandans with whom they

had spent their first winter on the trail. Here Colter left them to return to the wilderness. And here they parted with Sacajawea and her family, since Charboneau desired to remain among the Mandans. Clark writes: "I offered to take his little son, a butifull promising child who is 19 months old to which they both himself & wife were willing provided the child had been weened."

Lewis and Clark reached St. Louis at noon, September 23, 1806, announcing their approach by firing of cannon. All St. Louis, hearing the splendid noise, rushed down to the bank to greet them. The welcome, Clark says, was "harty." On the next day they wrote letters, Clark to his brother, Lewis to Jefferson; and Drouillard, one of the crew, sprinted off with them to overtake the mounted postman. The explorers then sallied forth to procure new attire, which they sadly needed. They bought cloth and took it to a "tayler." On the twenty-fifth they "payed" visits and in the evening were honored by a "dinner & Ball." The next day Clark jotted down the last line of the great epic: "A fine morning we commenced wrighting &c."

In 1807 Meriwether Lewis was appointed Governor of Louisiana Territory. Two years later, while riding along the Natchez Trace on his way to Washington and accompanied only by his servant, a Spaniard, he paused for the night at a lonely inn, seventy-two miles below Nashville in Lewis County, Tennessee. Here he was shot. For a long time the impression prevailed that he had taken his own life in a fit of depression. Later investigations, however, have led to the conclusion that he was robbed and murdered by the half-caste, Grinder, who kept the inn. But the belief of Lewis's family was that the Governor had been done away with by his Spanish servant, not only for the money on his person but for the sake of certain documents which Lewis was taking to Washington. Whether Lewis fell a victim to the rapacity of the ill-reputed Grinder, or whether his death was but one more knot in the intricate skein of Spanish intrigue, will now, probably, never be known. But, at least, the theory of suicide no longer beclouds his fame. His body was buried beside the Trace near the spot where death found him. In 1848, the State of Tennessee raised a monument of marble over the grave. Even today the scene is a wild one. Forest, uninvaded by axe or plow, closes about the broken column which marks the place of Meriwether Lewis's last sleep on trail.

William Clark survived his friend for thirty years. His was a life crowded with useful activities. A year after his return he entered the fur trade. He was appointed Governor of Missouri Territory in 1813 and retained the office until Missouri was admitted to statehood in 1820. Later he became Superintendent of Indian Affairs and held that post until his death. He had already, on his western journey, established among the Indians a reputation for courage, justice, and friendship. His influence with the tribes was probably greater than that of any other white man since Sir William Johnson of colonial days. The name of "Red Head" was loved and revered in every lodge and wickiup from the Mississippi to the Pacific. As Governor and as Superintendent of Indian Affairs, his executive ability, shrewd common sense, and his farsightedness, integrity, and humanity made his official acts constructive incidents in the growth of the American commonwealth.

In his personal relations he was loyal, affectionate, and generous. In behalf of his brother he addressed dignified and just appeals to the Virginian authorities for payment of the debts which George Rogers Clark had contracted in the equipment of his Illinois campaigns. And when

Virginia would not pay, and George Rogers Clark could not, William Clark assumed the burden. It was his insistence that won at last a small pension for his brother. He also paid notes of Lewis's which had been protested, so that the honor of his dead friend should not be smirched. We know that he did not wish to forget the Bird-Woman who had guided him safely to Three Forks on his homeward journey, since he offered to adopt and educate the son born to her on the march, and presumably also he was responsible for the appointment of old Charboneau as interpreter at the Missouri Sub-Agency in 1837.

William Clark married twice and was the father of seven children. His first wife was the lady for whom, as he supposed, he had named Judith River. He died in 1838, aged sixty-eight years, and he was buried in Missouri.

Clark lived to see great changes come to Missouri after the transfer of the territory to American rule. Then St. Louis was only a small village, backward in comparison with any American settlement of its size, and La Charette, some forty odd miles to the northwest, was the farthest frontier. But in 1838 there were many thriving American settlements in Missouri, and St. Louis was the emporium of a vast trade in furs, the arteries of which ran through that great wilderness first mapped and in part first explored by Lewis and Clark.

CHAPTER III

THE REIGN OF THE TRAPPER

THE fur trade of North America — which encouraged and sustained the earliest French and English explorations inland, which was the chief spoil fought for in the colonial wars, and which swept across the continent, the forerunner of colonization, to see the last days of its glory in Old Oregon — began as an accident. It was not furs in the first place that brought Europeans adventuring on the northern shores of the New World. Immediately in the wake of those earliest mariners searching for the pathway to the East came other sea rovers to fish for cod. This takes us back to Sebastian Cabot. Sebastian returned from the second English voyage to America — the voyage of 1498 — with marvelous fish stories, which so stirred the watermen of Europe that fishing vessels from England, France, and Portugal were soon on the Banks of Newfoundland. Presently Spaniards

THE REIGN OF THE TRAPPER 75

oined them, and it was not long before Basque whalers from the Bay of Biscay were wrestling with Leviathan in American waters. The French seem to have led all the rest, even as they were later to lead the way as trappers and fur traders.[1] The fishing fleets went out in April and returned in August. The industry was divided, then as now, into "green" and "dry." The dry-cod fishers built platforms on shore on which they split and dried their fish. Each ship had its own station to which its crew returned year after year. And these dry-cod fishers, who lived partly on shore for three months of every fishing season, were the first white men to trade with the Indians for furs.

We should not turn away too quickly from the picture of the first Indian who stepped forward to offer a beaver pelt to a man of our race in exchange for some trinket made in Europe. That picture illustrates the opening chapter of a great romance. The Indian's gesture beckons the white man to the free march of the forest trail and the rhythmic glide of the birch canoe. His beaver pelt is a sign

[1] By 1578 the French had 150 vessels off Nova Scotia and Newfoundland — as against 100 Spanish, 50 Portuguese, 25 Basque, and 50 English vessels — and in 1603, four years prior to the Jamestown settlement, they had nearly 600 ships on the Banks. See H. P. Biggar, *Early Trading Companies of New France.*

pointing northward, southward, westward. Al
trails lead to the beaver lands; and, in following
them, the trapper shall pierce to the Frozen Se.
and to the Ocean of the Setting Sun. And, besid
those great inland waters of which the old mariner
dreamed, his camp fire shall glow like a star dropped
upon the waste.

It was the French who first caught the vision o
the fur trade. The Dutch bartered with the In
dians at Manhattan and far up the Hudson. And
English traders were the first pathfinders across
the Appalachians. But it was Frenchmen who
in advance of all others, pursued the little beaver
into the wilds of the continent. If the goal they
sought was the legendary strait, their activities
were quickened and supported by the fur trade
It was as fur traders that Champlain and his associ-
ates explored the region of the Great Lakes. It
was the beaver that lured on Radisson and Groseilliers, the first white men to reach the prairies beyond the Great Lakes and probably the first to
pass overland to Hudson Bay. Again it was the
beaver that made possible the exploration of the
Mississippi by Joliet and Marquette and La Salle,
and the discovery of the Saskatchewan, and of the
Black Hills of South Dakota by La Vérendrye.

Before New France fell the French had established trading posts reaching from Montreal up the Great Lakes, across to the Lake of the Woods, on to Lake Winnipeg, and up the Saskatchewan as far as the Rocky Mountains.   By a chain of forts circling southward, from the head of Lake Ontario, they dominated the Ohio, the Wabash, the Wisconsin, and the Illinois.   They were on the Arkansas, the Red, the Osage, and the Kansas.   Through Kaskaskia, New Orleans, Fort Alabama, and their itinerant trade with the tribes from Tennessee to the Gulf, they were masters of the Mississippi.

For the Frenchman in Old Canada the life of the wilderness had an irresistible lure.   In vain the authorities at Quebec tried to compel him to live within the settlements and cultivate the soil.   The glamor of the woods drew him away to follow the beaver with the Indian trappers.   He married among the Indians and reared his children in their lodges.   Thus there sprang up that new and entirely unique type of man, the *coureur-de-bois*, or trapper, and his complement and companion, the *voyageur*, or canoeman — rovers of the forest; first offspring of France in the New World; speaking two mother tongues; care free and good-humored; disdainful of hardship and danger; and indifferent to all education other than the Indian's lore. The governor might ban them; the priest might deplore their impiety; but through them France wielded the first great fur empire of North America.

This, however, was not an undisputed empire. There was soon an English rival in the field — a rival for which two Frenchmen were responsible. It was in the summer of 1666 that those intrepid wanderers and traders, Radisson and Groseilliers, having fallen foul of the Governor at Quebec in the matter of trading licenses, found themselves — after a series of vicissitudes — in London. Out of ruin, persecution, and shipwreck, they entered into a city of gloom. London lay under the pall of the Great Plague. The gay monarch, Charles II, had fled to Oxford and was holding court there, surrounded by his favorite nobles and his best beloved ladies. But the King was bored; he found life at Oxford very dull; so he welcomed the chance of hearing the two French castaways tell their marvelous tales of adventure in the New World. He enjoyed their stories — thought them so good as to be worth forty shillings a week for the rest of the year, a very fair pension indeed for a couple of entertainers in those days.

By the winter of 1666–67 fire had swept London

clean of contagion, and the King and his courtiers returned to the city. Once in London and still under the royal favor, the merry monarch's two entertainers became the rage. Prince Rupert, the King's Admiral and cousin, just home from the Dutch Wars, was much taken with them. So were the aldermen and the high patrons of commerce; for, though the Dutch wars had given to England the Dutch colony of New Netherland on the Hudson, they had been disastrous to English trade upon the sea; and patriotic and practical Englishmen were looking all ways for means to recoup their losses. So Radisson and Groseilliers (the latter appears in the records as "Mr. Gooseberry") were invited to castle, tavern, and coffee-house to expound their views on the fur trade over roasted pullets.

This abundant feasting and story-telling had its *dénouement,* first, in a voyage to the shores of Hudson Bay to establish the verity of the Frenchmen's tales as to the trading opportunity in that region, which was English by right of Hudson's discovery in 1610, and, secondly, in a charter given under the King's seal in 1670, granting unto his cousin Prince Rupert and seventeen courtiers, designated as the "Governor and Company of Adventurers of

England trading into Hudson's Bay," in feudal
domain, all the lands drained by waters flowing into
that great inland sea.   This charter, giving away
an empire almost half the size of Europe, the King
signed with his quill pen.   He was richly garbed
for the ceremony in the new style of coat and vest
designed by himself.   He was in a happy frame of
mind, for now he had an antidote for the tantrums
of milady Castlemaine in the warm-hearted gaiety
of "pretty witty Nellie," as the diarist Pepys calls
Nell Gwyn.   Surrounding the King, as he affixed
his royal signature to the instrument, stood the
"gentlemen-adventurers" named therein, among
them the weak James, Duke of York, afterwards
King, and the martial Rupert, soldier, sailor, and
artist, a man of power, and the outstanding figure
of the group.   Had Rupert been King instead of
that pretty philanderer in the chair, perhaps the
course of these eventful years would have been
better for England.   But who can know?   What
one of that brilliant group imagined that the Company they formed would long outlive the Stuart
dynasty?   It was decreed that the territory granted
under the charter should henceforth be known
as Rupert's Land.   But, though the Company of
which Rupert was the first Governor still flourishes,

there is no Rupert's Land mentioned on any map of that country today.

The Company sent ships to Hudson Bay and built forts on the Nelson and Hayes rivers and on James Bay.   Yearly three vessels sailed from England with goods and returned laden with furs.   Unlike the French traders, the officers of the Hudson's Bay Company did not range the woods to trade but lived in feudal state within their stockaded forts and waited for the Indians to come to them. As a group of Indians approached one of the forts, the commander and his subordinates would emerge to greet them.   The commander wore a periwig, a sword, and a silken cloak.   His manner was courteous and aloof, his discourse dignified and straightforward.   The Indians quickly learned to know him as a man of his word and a trader who had one price and no rum.   This way of trading worked very well for a short time.   But one year it was noticed that fewer Indians were coming to trade; the next year there were fewer still.   The reason was soon learned.   Canadian traders, branching north from the St. Lawrence, were intercepting the tribes and getting their furs.

These Canadians, a company of stout traders and dare-devils as reckless and unscrupulous as ever ranged the wilds, saw that English frost on the shores of Hudson Bay threatening blight to the lilies of France. But this was the year 1686, and France and England were at peace. And could some hundred armed men pass through the gates of Quebec on their dash to Hudson Bay without the cognizance of the Governor? They could, if the Governor would look over his other shoulder. Beautiful indeed were the gates of Quebec to the eyes of every loyal Canadian; but were there not other fine views to be admired from the castle windows? Evidently the Governor thought so, for a raiding force was presently on its way overland to Hudson Bay. With the marauders, dressed as Indians, went three Le Moynes, young men in their twenties, one of them that Pierre Le Moyne d'Iberville later to win fame on land and sea as the most illustrious fighter of New France and as the founder of the colony of Louisiana which Jefferson was to add to the United States.

Swiftly, by forest, stream, and swamp, the raiders sped northward until they reached the outskirts of the English Fort Moose on the shore of James Bay. Lurking low in the shadows of the moonlit brush fringe, Iberville took note of the drowsy sentry. Then he darted forward, his moccasined feet

noiseless on the sod, and plunged his dagger through
the watchman's throat. The snoring traders within the fort woke to the firing of guns, the clink
of steel, and the yells of savage men leaping and
clambering over the bastions. Before the sleep
was out of their eyes, their fort was lost — and with
it their great packs of furs. Fort Moose was only
the beginning. All the forts on the Bay save one
were looted by the raiders, who then returned to
Quebec as fast as they could travel under their
burden of furs.

The Adventurers of England carefully transcribed
their losses in neat columns and doggedly set the
helm of their fortunes once more for the scene of
their disaster, only to meet again with the same
fate. One summer day, as the supply ships from
England sailed into the Bay against a stiff wind,
they spoke a vessel wafting out merrily under
full canvas with the Union Jack at her masthead.
Homeward bound! "A goode wind and a faire
sail to her!" They plodded on — to anchor before
forts looted and wrecked. It was indeed one of
their own ships that had sailed by them, packed
deep with furs; but the skipper of that ship was
Iberville, the raider.

Iberville made his last visit to Hudson Bay in

1697, before the Peace of Ryswick. Now that
France and England were at war, he wore, not the
fringed buckskin of a *coureur-de-bois*, but the uni-
form of a naval officer of France, and he commanded the *Pelican*, a French man-of-war. He
fought three armed English vessels on the Bay and
defeated them after a savage fight amid the ice-
floes. It was a strange setting for a naval battle.
Perhaps the furtive animals of the wilderness, hearing a sound roll in heavier than the roar of wind
and surf, stood still in their tracks and stiffened at
the thunder of that fierce fight for their pelts.

After the Treaty of Utrecht in 1713, when Hudson Bay was restored to England, the Adventurers
strengthened their half-dozen posts on the Bay and
built the great stone fort named Prince of Wales,
on the Churchill River.[1] This fort mounted forty-
two cannon — six to twenty-four pounders — and
was manned by some two score men. The rosters
of the other forts listed from eleven to forty men
apiece. And there in the bleak stillness and loneliness of the waste, year in, year out, these men
lived and traded with the Indians. They drank

[1] This fort was partially destroyed in 1782 by the French
Admiral La Perouse, as an ally of the Americans in the Revolutionary War. Its ruins are still standing.

snow-water for nine months of the year because the river was salt for twelve miles above its mouth; in the brief summers they hauled fresh water with three draft horses kept for the purpose. Their most pleasant duty, says one of them, was killing partridges.

But, in truth, very little is known of what happened during these years on Hudson Bay. When the last echo of Iberville's guns died away, a curtain of silence, thick and vast as the northern snows, dropped between the traders on the Bay and the bustling world. The records of the following years lie in the cellars of Hudson's Bay House in London; barely a hint of their contents has reached us. We know that yearly the ships came and went, bearing huge packs of furs home to London. We know, too, that gifts were made — silver fox tippets for Queen Anne, beaver socks for a George or two, "catt skin counterpanes" for some lordship's "bedd." Portly merchants and rich nobles, with their good dames, walked abroad in fur trimmings to stir the envious. Milord might be heard to say that he had paid a pretty penny for his beaver mittens — "egad, sir, yes, in good English money!" But little could he compute the cost of them. Behind that screen of silence was the true reckoning

made — where, at the short summer's end, the
white haze gathered and lowered and moved down
over land and sea, with a breath like steel, stilling
the waters, burying the land, piling white towers
about the trees, rearing white crags along the
shore, drifting against the doors of the trading
posts, shutting out the light of the windowpanes
with a white tapestry, dropping, dropping. "We
cannot reckon any man happy," said one, "whose
lot is cast upon this Bay." These were the cost
of milord's mittens — the monotonous life, the
loneliness of the silent years.

Meanwhile, far to the south of Hudson Bay, the
great struggle between France and England dragged
on. The Americans were pushing westward to the
tribes hitherto trading with the French. At length
the Governor of Virginia sent the young George
Washington to drive the French away from an
English trading post on the Ohio, where Pittsburgh
now stands, and the first shots of the Seven Years'
War cracked across Great Meadows. The conquest of Canada followed; and its bloody after-
math, the Indian rising called Pontiac's War —
which was the red man's protest against the new
masters of the interior trading posts, the English

colonial traders — ran its course. But the fierce struggle for the hapless little beaver was only beginning.

Out of the ashes of the old French fur trade, which was under governmental ward, arose a swarm of "free traders." Among them was a woods rover of a new type. English and French pursuing the beaver we have already seen. Now in the throng of the free traders the Scot appears. We shall find him presently taking the Frenchman's place among the Indians and rising to a leadership in the fur trade which he is never to surrender. He had his difficulties at first. The Indians in the old French hinterland distinguished only between French and English; and to them the Scot was an Englishman, one of a race they had been taught by the French to hate.

One of the first, if not the first, of the free traders to enter the old French country was Alexander Henry, the elder. In 1761 Henry went from Montreal to Fort Michilimackinac. This fort was a strategic point, as it commanded the route into Lake Superior, and was the chief depot for the furs from the territory comprising Wisconsin and Michigan. Here Henry was visited by sixty Chippewas, their faces blackened with war paint, and

tomahawks and scalping knives in their hands.
They consented, however, to trade with him and assured him that he might "sleep tranquilly without
fear of the Chippewas." This was a sweet promise
not long kept; for during Pontiac's War, two years
later, the same Indians, with some Ottawas, murdered the English at Michilimackinac and took
Henry prisoner. He was saved only by the friendly
offices of a Chippewa who had formerly adopted
him as a brother.

The "Handsome Englishman," as the Indians
called Henry, seems to have been the first British
trader to push beyond Michilimackinac into the
Lake Superior country. By 1767 his canoes were
on Lake Winnipeg. He spent sixteen years in the
wilderness and penetrated at least as far north as
Beaver Lake and the Churchill River. On the
way to the Churchill he traveled with three other
adventurers whose names are distinguished in the
fur trade, the Frobishers and Peter Pond.

It was not long, indeed, before the free traders from Montreal and Quebec were overrunning
the North and establishing themselves in Rupert's
Land — the sacred precincts of the Hudson's Bay
Company. The Frobishers built Cumberland House
on the Saskatchewan and Fort Isle à la Crosse

on the lake of the same name a little north of the junction of the Beaver and Churchill rivers. Both sites, commanding the waterways to Hudson Bay, were admirably chosen. At these forts the Indians going down to the Bay were intercepted and induced — by higher prices or by rum — to sell furs that were, in some instances, already paid for by the Hudson's Bay Company in credits. Up to this time the old Company had maintained its traditional aloofness, and, except for some notable exploring expeditions, it had not stirred inland from its forts on the Bay. But in 1774, Samuel Hearne, the Company's celebrated young explorer, discoverer of the Coppermine River, came up from the big stone fort at the mouth of the Churchill and built Cumberland House, on the lake of the same name. The old Company saw at last that it would be obliged to branch inland for the protection of its trade.

The free traders hurt the Hudson's Bay Company, but they hurt themselves much more — sometimes to the extent of killing one another. And their competition and their rum were disastrous to the Indians. Traders were murdered by Indians on the march; their forts were attacked and burned, and their goods were stolen. The precarious

condition to which the free traders at length reduced themselves is reflected in an official report to
the Governor of Canada on the fur trade, written
in 1780. This report says that, though the furs
are producing an annual return of £200,000 sterling,
the gathering of them is carried on at great expense,
labor, and risk of both men and property — every
year furnishing instances of the loss of men and
goods by accident or otherwise: that the traders in
general are not men of substance but are obliged
to obtain credit from the merchants of Montreal
and Quebec for each year's supply of goods; and
that, when their trade fails, they are destitute of
every means to pay their debts. [1]

It is not surprising, then, that the rival traders at
both Michilimackinac and Montreal took counsel
together and decided to put an end to ruinous competition. The Michilimackinac Company, formed
in 1779, was an association of thirty traders called
the Mackinaws. In the same year nine houses in
Montreal trading west of Lake Superior joined
forces; and four years later (1783) these Montreal
merchants, with some others under the leadership

[1] A report to Haldimand, dated 1780, signed by nine trading
houses of Montreal. Cited by Davidson, *The North West Company*, Appendix, page 256.

of the Frobishers and Simon McTavish, united in the partnership since known as the North-West Company, or the Nor'westers, the stormy petrels of the northern wilds.

The Nor'westers began in strife. Some of the "winterers" — partners who wintered in the great white land — were dissatisfied with the shares allotted them and violently withdrew. Among these was Peter Pond, explorer of the Athabaska and Great Slave regions, and too powerful a man to be left in enmity. His demands were speedily met, and he joined the Company. At this, the friends who had withdrawn with him were furiously incensed. They banded together and made war on the North-West Company's brigades. It became a war with powder and shot, for the Nor'westers stopped at nothing to smash their small rival. But when Pond killed Ross, a leader among the allied free traders, both factions took fright and united in haste to forestall any undesired investigation by the authorities. This beginning was prophetic. In the violence of their methods — and, be it said, in the brilliance of their achievements — the Nor'westers were to prove themselves deserving successors of the marauding and plundering Frenchmen on Hudson

Bay and also of the illustrious French explorers of Old Canada.

The majority of the partners were Scotch Highlanders; and it is not too much to say that they brought to their trade rivalry with the Hudson's Bay Company the spirit of Celtic chiefs at war. Their rival was a chartered company with a monopolistic grant, while they were only an association without royal favor. The Nor'westers, therefore, saw, as their first need, a loyal organization, every man of which should be bound to their interests by his own. Hence it was arranged that a clerk could become a partner after a brief term of service, the length of which depended upon his own initiative. Thus the Company attracted bold and resolute young men who were not minded to let fears or scruples shut them off from the coveted goal. The man who could produce results counted highest with the Nor'westers. Even some of the original partners contributed only their experience and energy: these were the "winterers" who commanded the trapping army in the field. The funds and the goods for trade were found by the partners resident in Montreal. But the real sinews of war were the *voyageurs* and the *coureurs-de-bois*, of whom the North-West Company employed great numbers. The servants of the Hudson's Bay Company were chiefly English and Scotch, who had first to learn the ways of the wild and so were no match for the Canadian boatmen and trappers, the product of several generations of wilderness life.

The Nor'westers made their interior headquarters on the north shore of Lake Superior, first at Grand Portage (Minnesota) at the mouth of the Pigeon River, and later at Fort William (Ontario) at the mouth of the Kaministikwia. These posts were outside the royal domain of the Hudson's Bay Company, but not far; only a day's journey over the watershed separated them from the Rainy Lake region drained by Hudson Bay and therefore Rupert's Land or Hudson's Bay Territory. From Grand Portage the Nor'westers' brigades ranged westward through Rupert's Land and far north to the Athabaska and Great Slave Lakes. They also tapped the territory south of Lake Superior and southwest as far as the Mandan towns on the Missouri. Nor did they wholly respect the regions to the southwest sacred to the Mackinaws, with whose men they frequently clashed.

To the *voyageur* of the Nor'westers' brigades there was only one person more ridiculous than a

Mackinaw *voyageur*, and that was a Hudson's Bay
man. The Mackinaw *voyageur* might be a great
man in his own opinion; but let him walk humbly
when men of the Nor'westers hove to at Michilimackinac for extra canoes on their way to *le pays
d'En Haut!* "*Je suis un homme du Nord!*" the
Nor'wester would brag as he jostled aside the despised Mackinaw. Anything to provoke a fight!
Like master, like man! Such discourtesies well reflected the views of the partners themselves towards their rivals in trade. The Nor'westers held
in contempt the Hudson's Bay Company, with
its slow ways and its code of lawful dealing. Its
pious principles — one price, no violence, and no
rum for Indians — the Nor'westers regarded with
unutterable scorn.

But let us see what these Nor'westers did to roll
back the mystery of unknown lands. Far to the
northwest, a thousand miles from Lake Superior,
stood their Fort Chipewyan, on the south side of
Lake Athabaska. There lived Alexander Mackenzie, a young Scot in his thirties, who had begun his
career as a clerk in a free trading establishment and
because of his abilities had been granted a partnership in the North-West Company. Mackenzie
proposed to make Fort Chipewyan not merely an

outpost of his Company's trade but the emporium of the greatest trapper's country on the continent. He saw the commanding position of his fort on Lake Athabaska as the central depot for a vast traffic. Great water highways led to it from every direction. On the south and west the inflowing streams of the Athabaska and the Peace linked him on the one hand to the Saskatchewan Valley and on the other to the Rocky Mountains. To the east lay a chain of lakes and streams stretching towards the rivers entering Hudson Bay. And to the north a tremendous river, issuing from Lake Athabaska, gathered up its mighty waters in the Great Slave Lake and moved on through the northern forests.

This river was unknown. Beyond the Great Slave Lake no white man had followed its course to the Frozen Sea. Nor had any white man yet penetrated the Rocky Mountains and reached the Pacific by land. Both these achievements fell to the glory of Alexander Mackenzie. In the summer of 1789 he discovered and explored to the Arctic the great river now known as the Mackenzie. And three years later, he passed up the Peace River, crossed the Rockies, and, on July 22, 1793, painted his name in red letters on a rock beside the Pacific Ocean.

Mackenzie's Odyssey was soon the gossip and song of the whole North. In Rupert's Land, building forts for the Hudson's Bay Company, was a young surveyor named David Thompson, who was greatly disturbed by it and discontented. He, too, wished to cross the mountains and explore. His ambition was to survey and map the whole of the great Northwest, to pierce the mystery of the wilderness with the clear light of science. But Thompson's pleas to the Company fell on deaf ears. He was too good a trader and altogether too valuable a man to send awandering. The North-West Company, however, would give him his opportunity if the Hudson's Bay Company would not. So it came about that Thompson, on May 23, 1797, being then at Deer Lake, wrote in his journal: "This Day I left the service of the Hudson's Bay Company and entered that of the Company of the Merchants from Canada. May God Almighty prosper me."

Thompson received his instructions at Grand Portage in June, the month after he entered the Company's service. He was to survey and map the fur country, showing the geographical position of the forts, and to find the forty-ninth parallel, which was to mark the boundary between the

American and British Northwests. He was to go south to the Missouri and explore the sites of ancient villages, hunt for fossils, and learn what he could of the ancient history of the country. For the rest he could follow his heart's desire; and his progress would be facilitated by orders on the trading posts for whatever he needed in men and goods. His was the biggest dream of all. Other men sought one river; but to Thompson the River of the West was only as a single brook on the great map he meant to make of the whole Northwest.

Thompson set out from Grand Portage, to be on trail almost continuously for nine years. In that time he ranged from Great Slave Lake to the Missouri, traced the headwaters of the Mississippi, entered the Rocky Mountains from the head of the Saskatchewan, made numbers of geographical sketches and scientific notes on the country from the Rockies to Hudson Bay and the Great Lakes, and surveyed the shores of Lake Superior.[1] His labors were by no means ended. In 1807 he

[1] "Thompson was an exceedingly accurate and methodical surveyor," says Mr. J. B. Tyrrell of the Geological Survey of Canada, the editor of Thompson's *Narrative;* "it was my good fortune to travel over the same routes that he had travelled a century before, and while my instruments may have been better than his, his surveys and observations were invariably found to have an accuracy that left little or nothing to be desired."

crossed the Rockies. He spent four years on the Columbia and its tributaries, building forts and trading with new tribes; returning to the Nor'-westers' forts east of the mountains from time to time with large packs of furs. He was thus the first man to make a detailed survey of those parts of Idaho, Montana, Washington, and British Columbia which are watered by the Columbia or by its source and branch streams.

A rare man was David Thompson — a little man, but every inch of him an inch of power. Except for his short stature he might readily have passed for an Indian with his jet black hair cut straight across his forehead, fringing his brows, with his black eyes, and his tanned cheeks painted with Nature's vermilion. An associate has left this description of him: "Never mind his Bunyan-like face and cropped hair: he has a very powerful mind and a singular faculty of picture-making. He can create a wilderness and people it with warring savages, or climb the Rocky Mountains with you in a snow storm, so clearly and palpably, that only shut your eyes and you hear the crack of the rifle, or feel the snow flakes melt on your cheeks as he talks."[1] In fort or on trail

[1] Bigsby, *The Shoe and Canoe.*

Thompson ruled his men like a benevolent master; and he was a law to himself, whatever the orders of his Company. He would have no liquor with his brigades; he would not use it in trade. Once two of the partners, Donald McTavish and John McDonald of Garth — whom we shall meet later — compelled him to take some kegs of whiskey for trade with the tribes in the mountains. Thompson selected a vicious, unbroken horse to pack the kegs and then let it go through the defiles at its own gait. The horse was in perfect sympathy with Thompson's ideas — only splinters of the kegs remained when the brigade reached the trading post — and Thompson reported that he felt sure the same costly accident would occur if another unwise attempt were made to transport liquor across the mountains.

Devoutly religious, Thompson sought the spiritual welfare of the *voyageurs* and *coureurs-de-bois* who traveled with him. He preached the moral life, a manhood sprung from the Godhead and confident in its source, brotherly and equitable, finding its joys not in excesses of the senses but in self-mastery. Seldom passed an evening in camp that Thompson did not read aloud three chapters from the Old Testament and three chapters from

the New, and then expound their meaning in
"most extraordinarily pronounced French." By
the rushing Saskatchewan, among the snow wastes
of Athabaska, on the bleak crags of the Rocky
Mountains, this prophet in buckskin, like Isaiah
of old, called to a primitive people, "Make straight
in the wilderness a highway for our God."

While Thompson was searching for the source of
the Columbia, another Nor'wester, Simon Fraser,
also exploring beyond the mountains, far north of
the Columbia, discovered the Fraser River and
followed it down to the widening of its mouth
near the sea.

The journals of Fraser, Mackenzie, Thompson,
and the elder Henry, like those of Lewis and Clark,
are records of heroism as well as of discovery; and
they are the earliest epics of the Great West. The
ideal of sheer manhood pitted against vast and
primal Nature, which is the underlying theme of
these journals, still animates the literature of the
West; but it is doubtful if any of the later writings
present that ideal more faithfully than do the
journals of these old explorers. Unconsciously,
out of his deep sincerity, Thompson makes himself
known to us as the Star-Man, the name given him
by some of the tribes, by day and night on the

plains and the mountains, taking observations with his primitive instruments, so that by the fixed law of the heavens he might at last bring the whole of that vast unknown land into the clear apprehension and, so, into the service of mankind. No finer touch of art than his is needed to picture for us this trader-astronomer and his small band of half a dozen men, almost out of food, pressing slowly and painfully through the dense snows of Athabaska Pass — where the dogs seemed to "swim in the road beat by the snowshoes," and, so high lay their route, that the stars looked to be within hands' reach — while somewhere behind them, as they knew, in close pursuit followed a warrior band of the fierce Piegans. Nor could literary imagination conceive of a more dramatic escape than the one he narrates without comment. The Indians came upon his trail in the mountains, and, perceiving the helpless situation of their quarry, knowing they had but to advance and kill, were stopped by the sight of three huge bears which emerged from the rocks and stood across the Star-Man's tracks. There the Piegans turned back, understanding that the Great Spirit had sent the bears to protect his son, for, as they said, "we all believe the Great Spirit speaks to you in the night when you are looking at the Moon and Stars and tells you of what we know nothing." One line from Thompson's pen lays bare the explorer's heart, when, following the mystifying bends and doublings of the upper Columbia, he cried out: "God give me to see where its waters flow into the ocean!"

There was another side to the life of the Nor'-westers. Whatever their lot, whether in fort or afield or in the countinghouse district of Montreal, they took life gaily. Their Beaver Club, on Beaver Hall Hill in Montreal, was a famous place. It was an exclusive club. No partner was eligible for membership in it unless he had spent at least one winter in the North. Men who had gone hardily through the rough life of a winter in *le pays d'En Haut* could be relied upon to keep the Beaver Club from stagnating, at any rate, and a right rollicking place they made of it, from all accounts, as they met o'nights to eat and drink, to toast the King and each other and all the lads of the North conglomerately and severally.

Spring was above all others the season of un-bounded joy, for in spring the brigades came in with their furs. Then it was that hilarity broke away from the confining walls of the Beaver Club and resounded through the streets and taverns of

Montreal and along the bank of the St. Lawrence.
On these nights, as April glided into May, fiddles
screeched and *voyageurs* and trappers jigged and
sang by the gleaming camp fires beside the river,
while some of their comrades sprawled on the
ground whiffing the beloved "tabac"; and betimes
Indian drums sounded under the scream of the
fiddles — like the undertone of booming surf in a
shrill wind — to the padding of the feet of Indian
trappers in the wild buffalo and wolf dances.

No less boisterous would be the scene in the
candle-lighted banquet room of the Beaver Club,
where sat lusty Scots wearing gold-braided uniforms, eating and drinking from silver salvers
and goblets, all engraved with the Club's crest —
a beaver — and the motto, *Fortitude in Distress.*
While from the river's bank rose the strains of the
voyageur's song —

> *"Lui-ya longtemps que je t'aime,*
> *Jamais je ne t'oublierai —"*

or the roar and bellow of the buffalo cry from the
trampling Indian dancers whirling with their pine-
knot torches, the revelers in the Beaver Club
poured still another libation to the lads of the
North. A McTavish or a McKay danced the

Highland sword-dance, to the plaudits and quaffings about the board.   Fortitude in Distress!   On two thousand miles of peril they had proved again that the brigades of the Nor'westers were manned by the swiftest, the hardiest, and the boldest men who roamed the wilds.   At length came the concluding ceremony, a tribute to the *voyageur*.   The lordly Nor'westers and their guests knelt on the floor and, with tongs, pokers, canes, or whatever would serve their purpose, imitated the canoeman's swift, rhythmic strokes, while they sang in rousing chorus one of his favorite paddle-songs.

When by river, lake, and portage the canoe brigades arrived early in summer at Fort William[1] on Lake Superior, even wilder scenes were enacted. The Nor'westers did not own Montreal; but Fort William was theirs, and at Fort William they made such laws and social conventions as pleased them. The fort held a huge banquet hall where two hundred men could feast at their ease.   Portraits of the King and of Nelson adorned the rough walls. But the picture most contemplated, no doubt, was the large map of the fur country drawn by David

[1] Built by the Nor'westers in 1803, on British soil, forty miles north of Grand Portage, their former Lake Superior headquarters, after some unwelcome visits from American customs officers.

Thompson. The fare on the rude tables was not inferior to that prepared in the Beaver Club, for the best French chefs, at lordly hire, had been cajoled to endanger their art and their lives on rapids and whirlpools in order to cook venison steaks and buffalo tongues to a king's taste in Fort William. To a Nor'wester's nice palate there was, it seems, nothing incongruous in a buffalo's tongue served up in one of those seductive sauces with which a Pompadour or a Montespan had once essayed to recapture the butterfly heart of her monarch. The finest of wines had also been carried over the long route to give tang to the welcome home. And, when the last drop was drained, the casks were rolled out on the floor and such Nor'westers as could still keep semblance of a balance would sit astride of them shouting and singing. Among the feasters were traders from the Far North — some of whom wintered on the Mackenzie River. Fort William was all that these outlanders ever saw of civilization. Here for a short time once a year they spoke with white men, ate and drank and clasped hands with their kind.

One of the events of this yearly gathering was the buffalo hunt. It was not only for pemmican and dried meat that the trapper hunted the buffalo.

He needed the skins for clothing and for bedding, for the making of his tent and bull-boat and saddle. The bone was put to various uses, supplementing the trapper's steel weapons; and the sinew sometimes served as thread or cord.

The trappers mounted and rode westward to their favorite hunting grounds in the country of the Mandans. Between the Saskatchewan and the Missouri lay one of the greatest buffalo ranges, where these animals roamed in such numbers that often a single herd was known to take several days to pass a given point; and the plains were plowed deep with their trails leading to and from their drinking-places. Sometimes the white trappers followed the favorite hunting methods of the Indian members of their fraternity, which were either to drive the buffalo over a cliff, for hunters stationed below to make an end of by rifle or bow and arrow, or to decoy them into a corral. This latter was accomplished by an Indian in a buffalo robe, skilled in the native art of mimicry. As a rule, however, the trappers preferred a fair field and no favor. They rode down on the herd, singled out their quarry, and fired the first shots that started the stampede. Then not only the hunter's skillful riding and his accuracy of aim but the intelligence

and speed of his horse were required to keep the
battle an even one.   For a stumble, a misstep, an
instant's slowness in wheeling and dodging, meant
death to the hunter and his mount.

After the hunt and, of course, the feast which
celebrated it the trappers prepared the meat and
skins for winter use.   All must now be made ready
for the time when they should set forth to trap.
Weapons were overhauled by the smith.   The
trapper's garments were cut and fashioned — by
his Indian wife, probably, for the gates of the fort
were wide open to the tawny belles of the plains.
Nothing too simple in style was considered good
sartorial art.   The trapper must have his moccasins plentifully beaded or worked with brightly
dyed quills, and his leggings and jacket must be
fringed.   He was forced to go without the little
bells or jingling bits of metal in which the canoeman rejoiced, for his task of stalking wild animals
necessitated a silent wardrobe.   But he could have
a bright sash, wonderful gauntlets, a beaded cap,
as well as a fur one for cold weather, fur pouches
for powder and shot, and perhaps a beaded bear's
or swan's foot pouch for his tobacco.   With these
added to his hunting suit, the trapper considered
himself appropriately tailored.   Sometimes a cap

mounted with horns or furry ears was included in
the trousseau in which he was to wed the white
Solitude. This was an Indian hunter's device for
deceiving wild animals where the man must cross
open snowy spaces to get within range. Other
methods also the trapper practised to conceal his
presence from the creatures of the wilderness.
When he set his traps, he trailed the hide of a
freshly killed deer over his tracks to obscure the
man-smell; and if he had handled his traps without
deer hide on his hands, he smeared them with an
oily substance extracted from the beaver, which
served also as a bait.

It might be that the gaily fringed and handsomely accoutered trapper, who set out with buoy-
ant heart as the snows fell, would return with wealth
in his pack. It might be that he would never return. The bait in his traps would lure other beasts
than the beaver or fox or mink he invited; and, to
the wolf-pack, the man-smell caused no fear.

While the Nor'westers were thus spreading the
trapper's kingdom towards the northern and western oceans, the traders of St. Louis were not letting
the time pass unimproved. Lewis and Clark had
opened the way for them to expand their trade

Not idly or casually had Jefferson instructed Lewis to form trading relations with the Indians along the Missouri. In the year after the return of the great expedition, Manuel Lisa, a Spanish trader, formed a partnership with Drouillard, who had been with Lewis and Clark, and ascended the Missouri to the Yellowstone. On the way he met the lone explorer and trapper, John Colter, and easily persuaded him to turn back. Up the Yellowstone they went, into the country of the warlike and pilfering Crows, to the mouth of the Big Horn. Here Lisa built a fort and opened trade. In the following year (1808) the Missouri Fur Company was organized with William Clark and Lisa as two of the partners; and in another two years the company had built trading posts in the Mandan towns and at Three Forks.

Not unhampered did the Missouri Fur Company's brigades, led by Lisa and Drouillard, pass upon the river highway; and it was believed by them and their friends that the Indians who fired volleys at their pirogues were set upon them by the Nor'westers to discourage the invasion of what those autocratic fur barons considered to be their territory. Drouillard, who was in charge of the post at Three Forks, was waylaid and killed by

Blackfeet while he was out hunting in the Jefferson Valley, in the year that the fort was built. Colter was captured by Indians of the same tribe. His courageous demeanor so impressed the Blackfeet that they gave the white man a chance for his life. Colter was stripped even to his moccasins, led out a hundred yards or so on to the plain and told to run. His run for life by which he miraculously escaped should long ago have inspired some maker of ballads. After a race of six miles over the plain, which was covered with prickly pear, he cast the Indians off his trail by diving under a raft in the river where he hid until the Blackfeet gave up the search. Then he swam downstream, landed, and traveled for seven days, naked, without weapons, his feet full of thorns, until he reached Lisa's fort on the Yellowstone.

The next notable figure on the fur-trading field was John Jacob Astor of New York. Astor was planning a vast scheme which involved the establishment of trading posts on the Columbia, a chain of posts across the plains—in fact, the control of the entire fur trade of the continent. He was acquainted with the Nor'westers, having bought furs from them for some years for his New York trade, and was anxious for them to join him in his enterprise on the Columbia if the matter could be

arranged.   As a preliminary step, he proposed that
he and they should buy out the Mackinaws and
thus remove a rival from the trade about the Lakes.
It suited the Nor'westers to help Astor obliterate
the Mackinaws, which was finally done, but further
than that his plans for mastery of the fur trade met
with no sympathy from them.   In particular they
disliked his views with regard to posts on the
Pacific Coast, for they were themselves about to
petition the British Government for a charter for
a monopoly of the trade west and immediately
east[1] of the Rockies; and it had been with this
purpose in mind that they had sent Thompson and
Fraser on their journeys of exploration.   Now appeared this cloud, Astor the American, on their
bright horizon.   The leading partners had a con-
ference with Thompson[2]; and although there seems

[1] Territory drained by the Athabaska and Mackenzie rivers
and therefore not within the chartered domain of the Hudson's
Bay Company.

[2] On June 28, 1810, Alexander Henry, the younger, at the
North-West Company's southernmost post on the Athabaska
wrote in his journal, "Mr. Thompson embarked with his family
for Montreal in a light canoe with five men."   Since Thompson
was traveling light, the inference is that he was speeding to Montreal in response to orders just received by the brigade returning
from that point, though he may have received his final instructions at Fort William on the way East and have gone no further.
His journals are silent on this point.

to be no record of it, there is little doubt that he was bidden to build a post on the upper Columbia and to lay claim to the territory about its head-waters and the Snake, and thence to complete his exploration of the Columbia to its mouth.   If his orders had been to beat Astor's ship, the *Tonquin*, in a race to the mouth of the river — as has often been stated — he would not have spent the spring of 1811 on its upper waters.   It was not by preceding Astor's men on the coast but by the charter they hoped to receive as a result of their explorations that the Nor'westers expected to gain Oregon, for as a chartered company they would be backed by the British Government.

Whether John Jacob Astor knew the plans of the Nor'westers, even as they knew his, is conjectural.   However that may be, he proceeded with his own enterprise.   His first contingent would sail in the ship *Tonquin* from New York and take the sea route round Cape Horn — the route which Robert Gray had sailed twenty years before — to the entrance of the River of the West.   And a fleet of pirogues, conveying men in his service, would strike from St. Louis up the Missouri to follow the trail of Lewis and Clark into Oregon.

CHAPTER IV

THE TONQUIN

If in these dawning hours of the Great West the trapper was lord of the land, the ruler of the waters along the Northwest Coast was the Indian hunter of sea-otter — a dark-skinned Neptune with spear for trident. The sea-otter trade, initiated by the Russians and advertised by Cook, had grown largely since the adventures of John Meares and Robert Gray. And it was almost wholly an American trade. By 1801 fifteen American vessels, nearly all from Boston, were trading with the natives on the Pacific; and in that year fourteen thousand pelts were shipped and sold in China at an average of thirty dollars apiece.

So it was that in the year 1810 John Jacob Astor of New York was preparing to capture the trade of the Northwest Coast, and the Nor'westers in Montreal were conferring with David Thompson to defeat him. That Astor had in mind the sea-otter trade when he decided to send a ship round the Horn, as well as an expedition overland, is not to be doubted. He would place the *Tonquin* in the sea-otter trade on the Coast and build posts for the land trade in beaver on the Columbia and at suitable points across the continent. Thus he would control a mighty fur-trading system reaching from the Great Lakes to the Pacific Ocean and on to China and India. It was a bold plan worthy of the genius and imagination of this pioneer of American commerce.

Meanwhile a similar idea had entered the Russian mind. In 1806 the Inspector at New Archangel, Alaska, had urged his Government to found a settlement at the mouth of the Columbia and to build a battleship for the purpose of driving the American traders away. His enterprising suggestion went further. He pointed out that, from the settlement on the Columbia, the Russians could advance southward to San Francisco and "in the course of ten years we should become strong enough to make use of any favorable turn in European politics to include the coast of California in the Russian possession." That the Russians planned to descend upon the Columbia in 1810, a Boston trader named Winship learned from his brother, also a trading captain; and he made haste to forestall them. Early in the spring, Winship ran his vessel up the Columbia, sowed grain, and began building on a low spit which he named Oak Point. Indian hostility compelled him to abandon the undertaking, and he departed with the intent to return next year in force sufficient to cope with the savages. Winship's attempt at occupancy amounted to nothing in itself, but his presence on the river that year caused a postponement of the Russians' secret design. But for this Boston seaman the story of Old Oregon might not now find place in the history of the United States. Two years later, in 1812, came just such a "favorable turn" as the forward-looking Inspector at New Archangel had been on the lookout for. While England was warring with Napoleon and Madison, and while Americans were intent on the conquest of Canada, an expansive Russia soundly established on the River of the West, with armored brigs to chase away American traders, might well have laid a locking grasp upon the coast from Alaska to California. Indeed, the War of 1812 had hardly more than begun when Russian traders stole down to Bodega, California, and, with the permission of the Spanish authorities, erected a trading post.

This trading post they subsequently transformed into a fort from which they refused to budge despite the indignant cries raised by Spain.

The belief prevailed among American traders that alien influences were at work among the savages. In 1803 occurred the seizure of the *Boston* and the massacre of the crew at Nootka by Maquinna's tribe. And in 1805 the savages attacked another Boston ship trading in Millbank Sound and murdered the captain and a number of the crew. Russian vessels were at this time cruising southward and were in the habit of calling at Nootka and at the mouth of the Columbia. No proof was advanced, however, of Russian complicity in these attacks.

It was plain that the time had come for a fort to be erected at the mouth of the Columbia — the time for occupation to attest ownership. On that subject, as we have seen, the Russians, the Canadian Nor'westers, and the American Astor were all agreed. The question was, *which of the three should build the fort?*

Of John Jacob Astor's early life not a great deal is known. He was born of poor parents in 1763 at Waldorf, a village near Heidelberg in Germany.

At sixteen he worked in a butcher's shop belonging to his father. Then he ran off to London. There, four years later, he learned that a brother had gone to America; and this news, coupled with his vision of money to be made in America, prompted him to try his fortune in the New World. It would seem that his thrift and his business acumen had already achieved results, for the young man who had arrived in London a penniless lad left for America on a ship sailing for Baltimore with a small collection of goods for trade. He reached New York some time in 1784. Here, following the advice of a furrier he had met in Baltimore, he exchanged his merchandise for furs and returned in the same year to London, where he disposed of his peltry at a good profit. He had found the right road to fortune. Ten years later he had established a profitable business and was purchasing furs in large quantities from the North-West Company of Montreal for shipment to Europe and China.

In 1808 Astor incorporated by charter from the State of New York the American Fur Company, with a capital of one million dollars supplied by himself. Soon afterwards he combined with the Nor'westers, as we have seen, to buy out the Mackinaws, whose American trade was turned over

to him with the proviso that he should not trade in
Great Britain or her colonies.   Astor's magnificent
plan was taking shape.   His acquisition of the
trading posts of the Mackinaws in Wisconsin was
the first link forged in the great chain which he intended to stretch across the continent and which
should bind under his control the whole fur trade
of the United States.   However little he knew of
the Nor'westers' ulterior plans, he saw that they
were spreading overland towards the Pacific; and,
wishing to eliminate them as rivals, he proposed
that they should join with him in the Columbia
trade and offered them an interest of one-third.
He was also planning to conciliate the Russians and
to gain control of the Pacific coast trade to China.
Probably he saw, in his invitation to the Nor'-
westers, the first step towards control of their
Canadian and British trade, also, and so, towards
ultimate mastery of the whole traffic of North
America in pelts.   And probably the Nor'westers
saw what Astor saw, namely, the final elimination
of themselves, even as by a coalition they had
helped him to eliminate the Mackinaws, for they
refused his offer and made swift plans for a descent
upon the Columbia.

Astor took up the gage of battle and went on

with the organization of his Pacific Fur Company for trade on the Pacific Coast. He believed that he would conquer his rivals and finally drive them from the new field beyond the Rocky Mountains. The Nor'westers had no sea-going ships. Their furs must reach Montreal from the West through Fort William by a long and perilous inland route; therefore, the farther westward they pushed their activities, the greater became their difficulties and their expenses in bringing their furs to market. On the other hand, Astor would have not only his cross-country chain of forts from St. Louis on the south and the Great Lakes on the north to the Columbia, but his sea-going *Tonquin* and in time other vessels as required. By sea, he would ship supplies to the forts on the Columbia, and from headquarters at the mouth of that river he would ship the furs to Canton, while his trading posts to be built along the Missouri would be supplied by pirogues from St. Louis and would, in turn, send their furs by the same means to that city.

Astor knew what was the chief factor in the spectacular rise of the North-West Company — its men. And he realized that, if his superior advantages in other respects were to count at their full value in the battle before him, he too must have men of the same stamina and experience. Where should he look for them? In the North-West Company itself, of course, for the Nor'-westers had no peers. He therefore opened the war by detaching from the Nor'westers several of their "winterers" and clerks. He enticed to join him, among others, Alexander Mackay, the great Mac-kenzie's companion in exploration, David Stuart of Labrador, and his nephew Robert Stuart, Duncan McDougal, and some clerks from Montreal, includ-ing Ross and Franchère, the authors of the diaries which are our chief sources of information con-cerning the enterprise. But Astor needed more than partners and clerks: he needed also some of those French-Canadian *voyageurs* who served with paddle and pole in the Nor'westers' canoe brigades between Montreal and Fort William. He enlisted into his service a number of these, and they came in a body with their canoes down the Hudson to New York.

Having recruited his men, Astor proceeded to carry out the first part of his plan, which involved making ready for sea his ship, the *Tonquin*, and sending it round the Horn to the Columbia, with several of his new partners and servants aboard. On the Columbia they would choose a suitable site and erect a fort, which McDougal would command, while the *Tonquin* under Captain Thorn would ply along the coast for trade.

The *Tonquin* was a vessel of some 290 tons, mounting ten guns and carrying a crew of about twenty-one men. Her captain, Jonathan Thorn, was a naval officer on leave of absence. He was a man of rigid determination, a believer in iron discipline, and easily moved to wrath by the smallest infringement of the hide-bound rules and proprieties of his code; a faithful, loyal man, but without the least understanding of human nature, and too lacking in imagination to have any sympathy or good feeling towards persons who were different from himself and whose characters, therefore, could not commend themselves to him. Thorn took his responsibility towards Astor very seriously. Doubtless he was prepared to die bravely and, if need be, go down with his ship in his employer's interest and for the honor of his flag. But what his employer's interests required of the skipper of the *Tonquin* was most of all humor and tact in dealing with the passengers. And neither humor nor tact was at all mentioned in any seaman's manual ever perused by Captain Jonathan Thorn.

He took one look at the "winterers" and their

voyageurs and despised them on sight for a shabby, roistering set of braggarts. He saw the partners sitting among the canoemen — no naval commander ever sat thus with deck-swabbers! — smoking with them, passing the pipe from mouth to mouth in Indian fashion (a custom which affronted his sanitary soul) and roaring with them in chorus the innumerable verses of *À la claire fontaine*, or *Malbrouck*. And he immediately wrote to Astor, in effect urging him to get rid of these noisy, useless knaves, who would do his project no good, besides being an offense to the eyes of a tidy man. When, at the first roll of the sea, partners, clerks, and *voyageurs* were overcome by seasickness, Thorn knew for certain that not one of them had ever done a man's job in his life. They were falsifiers and fabricators. They had never seen the fur country where they claimed to have experienced wild adventures; they had gone no farther into the wilderness than the waterfront of Montreal; they were waiters, barbers, draymen, and scallywags. He doubted much if any one of the *voyageurs* had ever dipped a paddle. In Thorn's experience, men who were accustomed to water did not get seasick. Yes, he had them there; it took a sailor to find these rogues out.

And what was the opinion of Thorn current among the ex-Nor'westers and their crew of paddlemen? We may readily imagine how the stiff and truculent naval dictator, with his set of rules, appeared to "Labrador" Stuart and to Mackay of Athabasca — Mackay, who had made those miraculous journeys with Mackenzie — men whose swift initiative had, time and time again, saved themselves and their comrades from sudden peril in the wilds. The *voyageurs* probably wondered by what right Thorn gave himself such airs, since all he had to do was to stand on the deck of a large stoutly made boat while the winds took it over the waves of broad open water without an obstruction. Put him in a frail bark canoe and let him run the boiling rapids, with great rocks, gnashing like the teeth of a devouring monster, to grind him to splinters. Would he, by a deft paddle-stroke, or a thrust of the pole, whirl his craft aside and send it flying past those jaws, like a feather on the spume? "*Crayez! Moi, j'n'l' crais pas!*"

Into this mutual non-admiration society Astor sent farewell letters filled with wise advice. The partners were assured that Captain Thorn was a strict disciplinarian, a severe man, whose favor they should cultivate by very circumspect behavior; and

Thorn was advised to prevent misunderstandings and to inspire the passengers with a spirit of good humor at all times. Here then was a setting and a cast prepared for either an excellent comedy or a bitter tragedy, according as circumstances should direct.

On September 8, 1810, the *Tonquin* was on her way out of the harbor of New York. That she was convoyed by the *Constitution* brings to mind certain facts and assumptions which have an oblique bearing on the subsequent history of Astor's enterprise. While the American Government did not take any part in Astor's venture, its attitude was sympathetic. It may be said that he had the Government's moral support in his large schemes for cornering the fur trade. And he had been readily granted an armed convoy to guard the *Tonquin* beyond the point where, it was rumored, a British man-of-war waited its chance to stop Astor's vessel and impress the Canadians aboard of her. The presence of the British vessel was supposed to be due to the machinations of the North-West Company. But that supposition hardly shows agreement in motive with another assumption, namely, that some of the ex-Nor'westers on board the *Tonquin*, McDougal in particular, were

still more loyal to their old company than to Astor.
To be impressed into the British Navy would have
prevented the opportunity they might have later
to play the game on the coast in the interests of
their Montreal friends. Some of them had already
related Astor's plans to the British consul in New
York; and all of them had deceived Astor in the
matter of the American naturalization on which
he had insisted. The British man-of-war is sufficiently accounted for by the fact that England, in
the midst of the colossal struggle with Napoleon,
needed seamen and was not over particular how
she got them.

All lights out and under convoy, the *Tonquin*
slipped by safely and headed south.

The salt air gave the passengers lively appetites.
They demanded food at all hours and cursed the
sea-biscuit that mocked palates yearning for venison steaks. Thorn's disgust increased daily. He
viewed with contempt the various clerks who sat
on deck scribbling down in their journals everything new to them that passed upon wave or sky.
Did the ship sail by an island that looked inviting?
At once there was a clamor to land and explore.
There was almost a riot on board because Thorn
refused to let his passengers off on the coast of

Patagonia where, so they had heard, the natives were of huge size and strangely made.

Occasionally it was necessary to make port because the supply of fresh water was low. The passengers would seize these opportunities to make explorations and to hunt penguins, sea-lions, or whatever game the coast afforded. And, paying no attention to the ship's signals to them to return, they would continue their amusement until it palled. The second or third time that delay occurred on their account — the ship was then at the Falkland Islands, in December — Thorn in a rage put to sea without them. Fortunately for the excursionists, the younger Stuart had remained on board. When Thorn refused to heave to and wait for the eight men who were desperately tugging after the *Tonquin* in the ship's boat, young Stuart drew his pistol and threatened to shoot the captain through the head unless he shortened sail and let the boat come up. A shift of the wind rather than Stuart's pistol slowed the *Tonquin's* pace and the indignant sightseers were presently safe on board. In Thorn's account of the matter to his employer, he deplores the shift of wind and asserts that it would have been to Astor's advantage if the men had been left behind. It is probable that this incident did little to improve the relations between the captain and the partners, for discord continued uninterruptedly throughout the voyage, waxing fierce off Robinson Crusoe's island in the Pacific, where the passengers wished to collect souvenirs.

On the 25th of December the *Tonquin* rounded Cape Horn and on the 12th of February put in at Hawaii and anchored in the bay of Karakakooa. Astor had given instructions as to the treatment of the natives of Hawaii, because he intended to establish trade with them. The ex-Nor'westers were thoroughly at home when it came to making the right impression on the Hawaiians. They had had experience in making friends with savages and knew that visits and councils and gifts, without haste, were the proper means. Thorn was interested only in securing a supply of hogs and fresh water for the ship, and he saw nothing but childish dilly-dallying in the conduct of his passengers with the natives. "Frantic gambols," Thorn called the whole procedure.

The partners had distributed firearms to their men, while at Hawaii, so that no possible act of treachery on the part of the natives should catch them unprotected. But Thorn suspected them of plotting to seize the ship. He had visions of a bloody mutiny in which he would be deposed, perhaps murdered, and Astor's enterprise would be ruined. He must have made his suspicion known, for the partners were soon playing upon it. They would make furtive signs, cease speaking English and converse in Gaelic, whenever Thorn came by. He wrote to Astor warning him about these "mysterious and unwarranted" conversations.

On March 22, 1811, the *Tonquin* stood off Cape Disappointment.

There was a high wind and a rough sea. On the hidden sand bars stretching almost across the entrance to the bay, the surf pounded and roared and leaped like Niagara. The ship hove to about three leagues from shore; and the Captain ordered Fox, the mate, with another sailor and three *voyageurs*, to take out the whaleboat and seek the channel. Fox begged for seamen to man the boat; but Thorn insisted that they could not be spared from their tasks on the ship. In desperation Fox appealed to the partners. They, in turn, argued with Thorn. The dangers were apparent. The whaleboat was a small ramshackle affair not fit to dare such a sea as now raced over the bar; the *voyageurs* were skilled in their special work as canoemen, but they had no knowledge of the sea. Fox was unfortunate in his emissaries. They merely stiffened the Captain's back. To Thorn, these were the men who had held his ship up while they hunted penguins, who had baited him in Gaelic and mocked his dignity with too much singing. Now they were trying to interfere with his management of his ship, were they?

At one o'clock in the afternoon the whaleboat left the ship. Those on deck watched it until it was hidden by the cataracts of surf. All the afternoon they waited for the boat's return with news of the channel. They waited through the night. Morning broke. The wind had slackened; the sea was calmer. The *Tonquin* sailed in nearer to shore. All that day the watchers on deck looked out hoping to descry the whaleboat emerging through the high roaring surf between the capes; and all day they saw nothing but the white hounds of the sea rushing at full cry across the bar. Darkness fell, and the ship moved out to safer water.

Next morning the *Tonquin* cast anchor near to the Cape. The pinnace was manned and lowered — Thorn could spare seamen today — and "Labrador" Stuart and Alexander Mackay went with the crew. The surf forced a retreat and Stuart and Mackay returned to the ship. Then Thorn headed

the *Tonquin* towards the entrance, but he dared
not attempt to find the channel through the piling
breakers. Once again the pinnace was lowered,
again to be driven back. Thorn sent it out a third
time with orders to sound ahead while the ship followed. Aiken, the seaman in charge of the pinnace, having found the channel, attempted to return to the ship at a signal from Thorn. The boat
was near enough to the *Tonquin* for those on board
to hear the cries for help that rose as the waves
suddenly swirled the little craft about and swept it
away towards the bar. Dusk was falling, and presently the pinnace was lost to view. The *Tonquin*,
still heading in, was in a perilous way. She was
striking frequently in the narrow channel and the
breakers washed over her. At length the tide rose
and the flow carried her in beyond the cape. She
dropped anchor in the bay.

In the morning, search parties were sent out
along the beach. Presently the party headed by
Thorn came upon Weekes, one of the men who had
been in the pinnace. His boat had been swamped.
He and a Sandwich Islander, one of the crew, had
reached land. Another Sandwich Islander's body
was washed ashore during the day. No trace was
to be found of the other white men who had been

in the pinnace, nor of the whaleboat and its crew.

The *Tonquin* had first anchored off Cape Disappointment on the 22d of March. Three days and nights had passed before those now aboard of her had looked over the safe waters of Baker's Bay behind the promontory. And eight men had perished.

There were clerks on board the *Tonquin* and they set down in their diaries, in detail, every incident of those seventy-two hours of terror. They wrote of the aspect of the coast, of the sound and fearful appearance of the breakers running mountain high, of the sunken bars that wreck ships. And after them came Washington Irving, man of letters. Irving read their journals and talked with other sailors who had adventured through the perils of that place; and he pictured faithfully, albeit discursively in the literary fashion of his day, the danger and the terror which Nature had set to guard the entrance to the River of the West. But our minds go back to the log-book of the discoverer of that river. And we begin to see the nature of the feat Robert Gray was recording when he jotted down those few terse sentences:

Being within six miles of the land, saw an entrance in the same. . . . At half past three bore away and

ran in northeast by east, having from four to eight
fathoms, sandy bottom; and, as we drew in nearer
between the bars, had from ten to thirteen fathoms,
having a very strong tide of ebb to stem. . . . At
five P.M. came to . . . in a safe harbor.

No; Robert Gray was not a writer. But he appears to have been a seaman.

Now began a series of squabbles between Thorn
and the partners concerning a site for the fort.
Thorn was for rigging up a shelter on the bay shore.
There he could deposit the stores and goods for the
trading post at once, and then be off up the coast
for sea otter. McDougal and the others, experienced in such matters, insisted on seeking a site up
the river where situation would offer some points
of natural defense. The site selected by McDougal
was on Point George about twelve miles up the
stream. Here was a sheltered harbor where small
vessels could anchor within fifty yards of the beach.
The *Tonquin* rode at anchor off the point, and the
Captain fumed as days and weeks flitted by while
the partners directed the building of the fort, with
its living quarters, storehouse, and powder magazine, or knocked off work to hold council with
inquisitive swarms of Indians led by their chief, old
Comcomly, the one-eyed. Since the one gentleman

was on ship and the other on shore, Thorn and McDougal could no longer match each other in spoken invective. So they sent splenetic epistles back and forth across the little stretch of water. By the end of May, however, the fort was completed. It was built of bark-covered logs and was enclosed in a stockade of log palings and mounted with guns after the model of the fur-trading forts in the North. In honor of John Jacob Astor it was named Astoria. On the 1st of June, the *Tonquin*, with Alexander Mackay and a clerk named Lewis aboard, took sail. A strong wind held her back within the bay for four days, but on the fifth she crossed the bar and turned northward towards Vancouver Island.

While the *Tonquin* was moving on her way and the men at Astoria were busy with their final touches to the fort and in planting various grain and vegetable seeds which they had brought with them, another fort was in building far up on the north branch of the Columbia at the mouth of the Spokane. The man who was building that fort was David Thompson, the Nor'wester.

In the autumn of the previous year (1810) Thompson had set out from Fort William to make his way to the Columbia. The natural route for him lay through the Rockies from the North Saskatchewan. But this pass was closed to him by the Piegans. He had been obliged, therefore, to ascend the Athabaska and to cross the mountains through the thick snows of Athabaska Pass. The crossing occupied weeks. It was nearly the end of January when Thompson and his men reached the Columbia near the mouth of the Canoe River. There they camped until spring.

In June Thompson was building his fort on the Spokane; and Indians were passing the news from village to village down the Columbia, till presently this spicy bit of wilderness gossip was retailed to the citizens of Astoria. The Astorians supposed that the men of whom they heard these tidings were Astor's Overlanders. But, one day in the middle of July, a canoe swept down towards the fort, with the British flag flying. McDougal and the Stuarts, who had rushed to the shore to welcome Astor's Overlanders, greeted instead the old crony of their grand battle days in Canada. Thompson was tossed from one rough embrace to another, then carried into the fort and, with his party of eight men, treated to the best that Astoria afforded. In consideration of Thompson's errand it has been customary to censure McDougal and the other partners for their reception of him; but on reflection it seems easy to take a more human view of the matter. It would require more than business rivalry or business loyalty to make such men forget what their long comradeship in the wilderness had meant to them in times when each had proved his claim to that "Fortitude in Distress," which had welded the Nor'westers into a clan, hardy and proud. Then, too, Thompson with his record of skill and success under enormous difficulties must have been a welcome relief to McDougal and the Stuarts after their long session with Jonathan Thorn, whose stupidity and obstinacy had sent eight lives into eclipse before ever a log of Astor's fort was laid in place. When Thompson ascended the river — which, now, he had explored from its source to its mouth — he was well provided with food and other necessaries. David Stuart, with several clerks and *voyageurs*, set out at the same time to find good sites for trading posts. And, when he and Thompson parted company, Stuart acted in Astor's interests and stole a march on the Nor'wester by choosing a site at the mouth of the Okanogan where he could compete for the trade which Thompson was expecting to attract to his fort on the Spokane. There Stuart established himself. Thompson in the meantime was faring north again through the mountains to put in the trapping season among the Salish and then to take the long route by lake and river to Montreal.

At Astoria the little colony now began eagerly to watch for the sails of the *Tonquin*. It was a watch kept in vain. The history of the *Tonquin* after she crossed the bar is barely more than a rumor, for the diarists at Astoria set down only so far as they were able to understand it the story told them by an Indian interpreter who was the only man to escape alive from the scene of disaster.

The *Tonquin* proceeded from Baker's Bay to Clayoquot on Vancouver Island. Here she dropped anchor and signaled for trade. This was done against the entreaties of the interpreter, who warned Captain Thorn that the natives of Nootka and Clayoquot were hostile and treacherous. Thorn was not one to listen to warnings. He was a courageous man, but he seems not to have been able to differentiate between fear and caution in other men. Not only did he insist on trading in that region, but he ignored all advice about letting the natives aboard only in very small numbers. He knew nothing of Indian character nor of the patience and tact which must be used in meeting their annoying methods of barter. One day, when Mackay had gone ashore, Thorn spread out the goods for trade and proceeded to tell the Indians precisely what he would give for each otter-skin. The natives understood neither Thorn nor his ways. They demanded more and still more. He refused to trade with them at all. His anger only served to arouse their mockery and insolence. One old chief, who had led the others in bidding up the prices, pattered about the deck after Thorn, poking an otter-skin at him and alternately quoting a price and hurling a gibe. In exasperation Thorn snatched the pelt and smacked the chief's face with it. Then he thrust the old native off the deck and kicked the furs about. The Indians gathered up their pelts and made for the shore in a fury.

When Mackay returned and learned what had taken place, he urged Thorn to set sail at once. Mackay knew the vengeful Indian temper. Thorn treated his counsel with contempt. Had they not cannon and firearms on board? Then why should they run from a band of naked savages? He refused to make any preparations against a surprise attack and turned in for the night.

Before Thorn or Mackay was awake in the early morning the Indians came alongside in their huge canoes and made signs to the man on watch that they had come to trade. They were apparently unarmed. As no orders to the contrary had been issued, the Indians were allowed on board. Canoes clustered about the ship with both men and women in them. The women remained in the canoes while the men clambered over the ship's sides. Mackay and Thorn hastily came on deck, and Mackay again urged the captain to weigh anchor. Thorn refused. The Indians offered to trade on terms satisfactory to Thorn and pelts were soon rapidly changing hands. The principal articles demanded in trade were blankets and knives. The blankets the men threw overboard into the canoes, but the knives they kept in their hands. As soon as each man had sold his furs and received his exchange, he moved off and took up a position on another part of the deck. By the time that the furs were all disposed of, there were several armed natives grouped advantageously near to every white man on deck.

The anchor was being weighed, men had gone aloft to make sail, and the captain ordered the decks cleared. With a yell, the Indians began the real work they had come there to do.

Lewis, the clerk, was stabbed in the back as he leaned over a bale of blankets and fell down the companionway. Mackay, who was sitting on the taffrail, was clubbed. He fell overboard and was received on the knives of the women in the canoes. Thorn made a fierce fight for his life. He was a big burly man of great strength, and he laid one or two Indians low with his fists and a clasp-knife before he was clubbed down and stabbed to death. Every white man on deck fell. There were seven men aloft. Four of them escaped by leaping through the hatch. They reached the cabin where they found the wounded Lewis. Here the five men barricaded themselves in, cut holes for their firearms, and began pouring out a fire that drove the natives back to their canoes and to the shore.

During the night the four men who were unhurt lowered the ship's boat and stole out upon the tide, with the desperate resolve of trying to row back to Astoria. When morning came the Indians, reconnoitering from a safe distance, saw a white man on deck. It was evident that he was badly hurt and very weak. He made friendly signs to them, inviting them on board. The opportunity for rich plunder was too alluring to be resisted. Presently a few natives climbed over the taffrail. The deck was empty save for the furs, the bales of blankets, and other merchandise. The one survivor had crawled below again; and there was no sign of the other men whose musket fire had driven off the savages after their victory of the preceding day. They signaled to their tribesmen who were lingering at a safe distance. And it was not long before the deck was thronged with Indians, while crowded canoes, rocking on the tide, rubbed against the ship's sides.

But, if yesterday had seen an Indian's vengeance, today was to see a white man's. Satisfied at last with the numbers of his foes which he had lured on board the *Tonquin* and about her, this sole survivor dragged himself to the powder magazine. The natives on shore heard a sound new to them and more terrible than the roar of the Thunder-God; it was the one note of a dying white man's war song. The *Tonquin* was blown into slivers by the explosion and the bay was strewn with bits of what had once been human bodies. Of over a hundred warriors who had been jauntily gathering the spoils on deck, only a few gruesome traces were washed ashore. Those in the canoes also suffered havoc. A number were killed; many were wounded and mangled.

There was mourning in Clayoquot. The death

fires burned along the shore; and wailing was heard in the great cedar houses which, last night, had echoed to the savage chant of triumph.

But a day or so later the sea cast up to the Clayoquots a sacrifice to appease the spirits of their slain. The four seamen who had left the *Tonquin* in the mad hope of reaching Astoria were captured as they slept in a cave. They were dragged to the village and were put to death after prolonged torture.

In substance, this was the story which the interpreter told to the Astorians when at last he arrived at the mouth of the Columbia with an Indian fishing fleet. Rumors had already reached the little colony by other Indians from the Strait of Juan de Fuca, who had come to the bay for sturgeon fishing. Indian gossip credited the Russians with having instigated the attack on the *Tonquin*. Indeed, the Indians still maintain that the attacks on American ships in those years were due to Russian influence.

The story of the *Tonquin's* fate and the depletion of the little colony, through the departure of Stuart and his party to the new inland trading post, moved the Indians on the lower Columbia to ask themselves whether they really desired the presence of the white men at Astoria. The vote was in the negative. McDougal knew Indians. Therefore he was quickly suspicious when he found them unwilling to trade and, in fact, deserting the fort where they had so recently made themselves very much at home. He set his men to work at once, strengthening barricades, putting guns in place, and making other preparations against attack. Then, all being in readiness, McDougal sent for Comcomly and other headmen, charged them with their perfidy, and vowed a terrible vengeance if they did not immediately mend their ways. He knew how terrified the natives were of the smallpox, which they believed to be the work of a devil. McDougal held up a corked bottle, declaring that it contained the spirit of the smallpox. Unless they behaved he would let loose that disfiguring and devastating devil. Hastily they assured him that they would behave. He was the greatest of all great chiefs. They would certainly behave.

McDougal, as time went on — so we learn — thought it best not to rely entirely upon the supernatural. Suppose a jealous medicine man were to steal the bottle and drop it to the bottom of the river? Such a contingency was not at all improbable. For the cement of good-will natural means would serve better than supernatural in the long run. So at last there came a day when the old Nor'wester girded himself with amity and put fair words in his mouth and went a-wooing. After sufficient gifts and palaver had been exchanged, one of the many Misses Comcomly became Mistress McDougal.

Presumably the marriage was a happy one, for it inspired other Astorians to seek connubial bliss. And, in time, old Comcomly, the one-eyed, came to be known as "the father-in-law of Astoria."

CHAPTER V

ASTOR'S OVERLANDERS

THE story of Astor's Overlanders is a tale of heroism which enriches history even while it reveals deplorable ignorance and inefficiency. Here, as in his maritime enterprise, Astor showed unwisdom in his choice of a leader. His own lack of actual experience beyond the frontier was most unfortunate for him, for it led to fatal mistakes in judgment. Apparently he could discern men's moral qualities, could perceive strength of will, courage, rectitude. Jonathan Thorn had possessed these traits, and they were conspicuous in Wilson Price Hunt, the leader of the Overlanders. But Thorn's inadaptability completely offset his good traits and brought about disaster. And Hunt's ignorance of wilderness life came near to wrecking the overland expedition.

In July, 1810, Hunt went to Montreal to engage a brigade of *voyageurs*, taking with him Donald

Mackenzie, a fellow partner in Astor's Pacific Fur Company, formerly a Nor'wester. At Montreal Hunt and Mackenzie found the hand of the Nor'-westers everywhere against their efforts to recruit rivermen and they failed to enlist the crew they needed. They took what they could get, however, and headed up the Ottawa and across Lake Huron to Michilimackinac, there to augment their force from the horde of idle boatmen and trappers who lay about the strait every summer waiting for the trapping season. At Michilimackinac, too, Hunt and Mackenzie experienced difficulties. No sooner was a canoeman engaged and a sum in advance paid to him than some tavern-keeper or trades-man would appear with a bill against him. Hunt must either pay the bill, or lose his employee and the money advanced to hold him to his bargain. Another cause of delay, quite as irritating, lay in the volatile temperament of the Canadian canoe-man. After Pierre or François had made his bar-gain and received his advance wages, he must celebrate — gather his friends and kin about him, carouse with them, sing and dance. Tomorrow, next day, or next week, would be time enough to embark; but today the wineshop beckoned, tonight the fiddles called.

10

At length the partners, with their train of vagabonds, were ready for the journey to St. Louis, across Lake Michigan, across Wisconsin, and down the Mississippi. They arrived at St. Louis on the 3d of September. Here Hunt, seeking to engage hunters and river boatmen, found Manuel Lisa of the Missouri Fur Company not one whit behind the Montreal traders in putting obstacles in his way. By the time that Hunt had manned and outfitted his expedition, it was too late in the year to set out; for the upper waters of the Missouri would be under ice before the boats could traverse more than the first five hundred miles of the river. But, apart from the expense of wintering sixty men in St. Louis, Hunt did not intend to leave his mercurial rivermen for months within reach of the taverns and of the machinations of the fertile Lisa. Towards the end of October he pushed far up the Missouri with his crew to the mouth of the Nodaway some miles above the site of St. Joseph. On this favorable spot in a good game country the Overlanders went into camp. Two days later the first blasts of winter closed the river immediately north of them.

In January, 1811, Hunt returned to St. Louis. He was anxious to engage more hunters, expert riflemen who might be needed not only to hunt game but to defend the expedition from hostile Indians. And he must also procure an interpreter to ease the party's way through the Sioux country where, according to report, he was likely to meet with serious trouble. On this quest Hunt encountered new difficulties, for the Missouri Fur Company was also equipping an expedition not only for trade but to make a search for one of their partners, Andrew Henry, who had been forced by the savage Blackfeet to abandon the Company's fort at Three Forks. Thus there was a lively competition for riflemen, in the midst of which Hunt was anything but gladdened to see five of his own hunters from the camp on the Missouri trudge into St. Louis. They had quarreled with the partners in charge of the camp. Hunt could persuade only two of them to return with him.

Hunt's pirogues put out from St. Louis on the 11th of March. Despite his setbacks, he felt himself fortunate in having the services of Pierre Dorion, a half-breed, whose father had served Lewis and Clark as interpreter among the Sioux. Pierre Dorion had been an employee of the Missouri Fur Company, but had fallen out with Lisa over a whiskey bill. Pierre considered it an unpardonable wrong that Lisa had charged whiskey against him at ten dollars a quart. Therefore he engaged with Hunt the more willingly. But as Lisa must pass through the Sioux territory, he, too, had urgent need of Dorion, the only man available knowing the Sioux tongue. When blandishments failed to detach the half-breed from his new employers, Lisa quietly secured a writ relative to the whiskey debt and arranged to have Dorion served with it at St. Charles, on the way up the river. Thus the interpreter would be prevented from continuing with Hunt, and must take his choice of either joining Lisa's own party or remaining in durance vile and penniless in the little village of St. Charles. Lisa's scheme was foiled, however, by two English scientists traveling with Hunt, named Bradbury and Nuttall, who had in some way learned the plot and who warned Dorion. The enraged interpreter left the boats shortly before St. Charles came into view and slipped into the woods, promising to rejoin the brigade on the next day at a safe distance above the village.

At the moment of departure from St. Louis, Dorion had given Hunt an unwelcome surprise; he had arrived on the river bank with his Sioux wife and two small children and had refused to embark without them. Now, as he left the boats below St. Charles, his wife and children and a bundle containing all his earthly goods went into the woods after him. But it was a lonely and disconsolate man who signaled from the shore the next morning. There had been a family tiff during the night and Pierre, always forcible in argument, had applied the logic of the rod. His wife, convinced but offended, had stolen away in the darkness taking with her the children and the bundle. Pierre's woe was so deep that Hunt halted the boats and sent a Canadian *voyageur* into the woods to seek for the lost woman, but without avail. On the following morning before daybreak, however, the distressed husband heard the voice of love calling to him from the opposite shore and woke the camp to share his joy. Hunt sent a canoe across; and the wife, the children, and the bundle were once more restored to their owner.

Hunt's next stopping point was the village of La Charette, at the mouth of Femme Osage Creek, the home, it will be recalled, of Daniel Boone, the famous Kentucky hunter, fighter, and explorer. Despite his seventy-five years, Boone had spent the preceding winter in the wilds trapping beaver and had returned with over fifty skins. Perhaps only the influence of his sons and his wife kept him from casting in his lot with Hunt's party. The old pioneer stood on the bank as the boats pushed up the river and watched them out of sight.

Early on the next day the Overlanders saw a small bark canoe with a single occupant skimming down the tide. It was John Colter, returning to civilization after one of his lonely trapping forays in the Yellowstone. He had much to tell the Overlanders of the malignant Blackfeet; and though he was strongly tempted to join their great adventure, the charms of a newly wedded bride, who awaited him somewhere down the river, appealed to him at that time more than the lure of the wilderness.

Passing through the territory of the Osages, the Overlanders learned that there was war throughout the greater part of the Indian country; and that the Sioux had been out on raids during the preceding summer and could be expected to take the warpath in full force as soon as spring had cleared the prairies of snow. They heard, too, that the Sioux had determined to stop white traders from selling arms to other tribes with whom they were at war. And while the boats halted at Fort Osage, where they were greeted by Ramsay

Crooks, one of the partners from the Nodaway camp, they saw proof of the rumors of Indian unrest. A war party of Osages returned from an attack on an Iowa village and held high festival to celebrate the taking of seven scalps. There were dances, with triumphant shoutings, processions, and planting of the war pole by day, and torch-light processions and barbecues by night.

These excitements so thrilled the still undis-ciplined savage nature of Dorion's Indian wife that, when the hour for sailing came, she declined to go on; she would remain forever where such pleasant things were happening. Dorion, how-ever, who had not forgotten the pangs which her absence had caused him earlier in the journey, was in no mind to go lamenting and lonely all the way to Astoria. He resorted again to the birch. Before Hunt could interpose, Dorion had convinced his mate that trivial amusements were not worthy to weigh against the duties and delights of matrimony.

By the middle of April the Overlanders joined their comrades at the mouth of the Nodaway, and, after a delay of some days, owing to the weather, they all started up the Missouri on their long journey to the Columbia. In the party, numbering about sixty, which Hunt was to lead, were four partners besides himself, and these four were experienced frontiersmen. Donald Mackenzie, one-time Nor'wester, was a "winterer" of the Great North; Ramsay Crooks, a Scot, had traded and trapped on the plains with Robert McLellan, an old border fighter famed for his exploits and his marksmanship; and Joseph Miller had fought as a lieutenant under "Mad Anthony" Wayne. To any one of these men might Astor more wisely have entrusted his overland expedition. Mackenzie, indeed, had joined with the understanding that he was to share the command. But at the last minute Astor had reduced to a subordinate position the bluff Nor'wester who knew the wilderness as Astor knew his garden. Then there were the hunters, among them the Virginian John Day, a clerk named John Reed, the interpreter Dorion and his family, and the crew of *voyageurs*. On the 28th of April they camped at the mouth of the Platte River for breakfast. Here they saw more signs of Indian war. On the bank lay the frame of a bull boat. It had been used not long since to convey a raiding party across the river. Rolling smoke on the horizon and, at night, a red glare in the sky told of grass fires lighted by a fleeing band to cut off pursuers.

A few nights later as the party slept, save the guards, eleven Sioux warriors rushed into the camp yelling and brandishing tomahawks. Seized and overpowered, they protested that their visit was friendly. But Dorion, being familiar with Sioux customs, said that their naked state showed them to be members of a band defeated in war who had cast off their garments and ornaments and vowed to recover their honor as warriors through performing some act of blood. But for the prompt action of the guards the eleven devotees would there and then have retrieved their right to flaunt feathers. Hunt sent them across the river towards their own territory under ward of his riflemen, with a warning. He was not in a mood to appreciate Indian pleasantry of that nature. Two more of his hunters had deserted only a couple of days before. If they continued to desert as the need of them became greater, the situation promised to be serious enough. These frequent desertions by hunters inured to the wilderness and its dangers are in strong contrast to the loyalty and obedience of the men who served under Lewis and Clark. This is accounted for by Hunt's ignorance of the men he was dealing with. Apparently he knew neither how to allay grievances nor how to enforce law.

Lewis and Clark, themselves experienced in frontier life, could give initiative full play without relaxing the bonds of discipline.

Hunt had other anxieties. It will be remembered that two English scientists were traveling with the expedition. Bradbury, an elderly botanist and mineralogist, had been sent out by the Linnæan Society of Liverpool to make a collection of American flora. Nuttall, a younger man, was also a botanist. Bradbury carried a rifle, for he was a mild sportsman after the manner of English country gentlemen of his day; but Nuttall's sole weapons appear to have been his microscope and trowel. At every halting place, regardless of the Indian danger, the two scientists would wander off over the prairie in different directions each absorbed in his special pursuit. Did Nuttall discover a new plant, or Bradbury overturn a bit of mineral stone, instantly all warnings were forgotten. They would range farther and farther afield until recaptured by a band from their own party. Nuttall, armed only with his trowel, tripping out over the Indian prairie to dig for roots that were not for the pot, especially drew the amused contempt of the *voyageurs*. They called him "the fool." *Où est le fou?* became a byword of the camp.

One day, as the boats approached a bend in the river, Bradbury elected to leave his boat and walk across the stretch of prairie which lay in front of them. They were in the country of the fierce Teton Sioux, who were gathering in force, Hunt had just learned, to bar their progress and take away their goods and weapons. In vain Hunt reminded Bradbury of "Indian signs." Bradbury had seen "signs" of iron ore. With the huge portfolio in which he pressed flowers under his arm, his camp kettle slung on his back, and his rifle over his shoulder, he set off. This day the old gentleman met with an adventure. After having emptied his rifle noisily but ineffectively at some prairie dogs, he stood near the bank at the upper side of the bend peering at a mineral specimen through his microscope when he felt ungentle hands upon his shoulders. There ensued a few lively moments during which three or four savages alternately threatened him with a leveled crossbow and tried to drag him away to their main camp. Against their carnal weapon Bradbury opposed the arms of science. The crossbow was lowered before the charms of the scientist's pocket compass. When the novelty of the compass wore off and hands again descended on Bradbury's shoulders, he produced the microscope. The fascination of this instrument fortunately held the attention of the Indians until the boats came up, when they fled.

The Indians visited the camp next day with a white man bearing a note from Manuel Lisa asking Hunt to wait for him so that the two bands might pass together through the Sioux country. In view of his experience of the Spaniard and his methods, Hunt did not regard the overture favorably. Moreover, he had heard from Ramsay Crooks and Robert McLellan of treachery which they believed to have been dealt them by Lisa in the previous year in the Indian country. Hunt decided not to wait. He sent Lisa an ambiguous, though a friendly, answer.

On the morning of the 26th of May, Hunt was deploring the loss of two more deserters when two canoes bearing white men hove in sight. The men were three hunters, Robinson, Hoback, and Rezner. They had been with Lisa's partner, Andrew Henry, on one of the head branches of the Columbia, where Henry had gone after the Blackfeet had driven him from the Three Forks of the Missouri. They were Kentuckians of the stripe of those great frontiersmen who won and held the Dark

and Bloody Ground. Robinson was a veteran of
sixty-six years. He had been scalped in the Kentucky wars and wore a kerchief about his head
to conceal his disfigurement. The three were on
their way home to Kentucky; but, learning what
was afoot here, they turned their canoes adrift
on the stream and threw in their lot with the
Overlanders.

A few days later the expedition confronted a
Sioux war party some six hundred strong gathered
on the river's bank. The Overlanders hastily
loaded swivel guns and small arms and made ready
to fight their way through. The Sioux, seeing
these preparations, spread their buffalo robes on
the ground — their sign of peace, as Dorion explained — and invited the white men to a council.
Hunt, with the other partners and the interpreter,
stepped ashore — followed, it should be added,
by the elderly scientist, Bradbury, who was
always eager to collect data concerning the abo-
rigines. The calumet was passed round the circle
and presents of tobacco and parched corn were
brought from the boat. The demeanor of the
white men was friendly and the gifts stacked beside
Hunt were appetizing. And the warriors could
see the hunters with their rifles on board the boats,

while the swivel guns pointed shorewards like fingers of benediction lifted over the peace council. The chiefs declared that they had meant to interfere with the white men's boats only because they believed they were carrying ammunition to the Arikaras, Minnetarees, and Mandans, with whom the Sioux were now at war. Since the white men were merely on their way to join their friends beyond the mountains, the Sioux had nothing but kindly feelings towards them.

Two days had barely passed when another large Indian band was sighted running down to the river as if to seize the boats in the channel ahead, which was narrowed by a sand bar. Immediately the men crouched low, their rifles ready. Miller felt a touch on his arm. Nuttall had risen to his feet and was peering at the flock of feathered warriors. "Sir," Miller heard the scientist ask with much animation, "don't you think these Indians much fatter and more robust than those of yesterday?" These fatter Indians, however, proved to be Arikaras and their allies, out for a skirmish with the Sioux. They jumped into the water and held out their hands in the way of the white man's greeting, and then hastened away to their towns up the river to prepare their people for the visit of the white

traders with the hope, of course, of a supply
of arms.

The expedition was still some miles below the
Arikara village when two Indians came up in haste
to inform Hunt that another large trading boat
was ascending the river. Manuel Lisa had read
between the lines of Hunt's soft answer and was
straining every nerve to overtake Astor's barges.
Hunt thought it best to lie to and wait for the
Spaniard. He seems to have spent the waiting
time chiefly in calming the fiery McLellan, who
had sworn to shoot Lisa on sight because of the
Spaniard's machinations against himself and his
partner Crooks among the Sioux the year before. Another member of Hunt's party whose soul
turned to gall at the prospect of Lisa's society was
Pierre Dorion. He remembered now not only the
ten-dollar whiskey, not only the threat breathed
into his ear in St. Louis, but also the sneaking
writ that had been intended to lay him by the
heels in St. Charles; and probably he charged up
against Lisa those distressful hours spent without his adored mate and his children and his bundle. Brooding on his wrongs, Dorion sank into a
sullen rage.

The Overlanders were traveling in four boats.

Lisa's party, which numbered twenty-four besides himself and a young sightseer named Henry Brackenridge, had one large boat, propelled by twenty rowers and mounting a swivel gun on the bow. Among this boat's occupants there sat a woman and her child — no other than the Bird-Woman, Sacajawea, and the small boy who had entered into the world while his heroic mother was on the march with Lewis and Clark. As on that journey, she accompanied her husband Toussaint Charboneau, the interpreter. The great event of her life, the crossing of the continent with Lewis and Clark, and the characters of those two brave adventurers had impressed the Bird-Woman with a deep love for the white race; and she had tried, in her humble fashion, to imitate their ways of life as far as she was able. But now, it seems, she was ill, perhaps drifting into a decline as do so many Indians after contact with the alien white people; and her desire was towards her own tribe, the far distant Shoshones, that her days might be finished among them. This will be our last glimpse of the intelligent and courageous Bird-Woman, who piloted Clark safely through the mountain passes on the homeward march.

And what of the little Charboneau, at this time about six years of age?   Casting forward throughout some forty years, we find references to him in the annals of Oregon and Idaho traders.   It appears natural enough that he should have struck out for the country of his mother's people and for that farther West of her wonderful journey, for these were surely the subjects of most of the stories she had told him in his childhood when they two sat in the fire's gleam and she spun for him the magical threads of romance, as mothers do all the world over.

For two days the rival traders traveled together in apparent good-will.   Lisa, indeed, was so smooth-tongued and gracious that Dorion forgot his wrongs and accepted an invitation to visit the Spaniard's boat.   Lisa plied the half-breed generously with whiskey and sought to win him from his allegiance.   But Dorion had his own sense of honor; and not for bribes nor even for the liquor he too dearly loved would he consent to break his agreement.   Lisa must have lost his temper at this inconvenient exhibition of rectitude, for he threatened to retain Dorion, forcibly if need be, to work out his old debt of ten dollars a quart.   Dorion flew into a rage, left the boat, and went to Hunt at once with the story. Lisa followed him but was not in time to prevent Dorion's revelations, if that were his object. There was a violent scene; and Dorion, whose blows were always readier than his words, struck Lisa. The noise of the brawl presently lured all lovers of excitement to the spot. Lisa had a knife, but Dorion seized a pair of pistols and so kept his foe at a distance. McLellan came up with his rifle, and Hunt had some difficulty again in persuading him to defer the payment of his vow.

Meanwhile the scientific Bradbury and the literary Brackenridge were doing their best to aid Hunt in soothing the combatants. Lisa, in his spleen, next hurled an insult at Hunt. Hunt's ire rose, and he challenged Lisa to a pistol duel. Both expeditions might have come to a permanent halt that night, had Bradbury and Brackenridge not succeeded in preventing the duel from taking place. It was Lisa who yielded. He realized, no doubt, that, if he fought Hunt and won, he would have Dorion and McLellan to settle with afterwards.

The two expeditions continued in company during the days following, but there was no further interchange of courtesies until they arrived before the Arikara village and pitched their camps

on opposite shores near the mouth of the Grand
River (South Dakota). Lisa then sent Brackenridge to Hunt's tent with the suggestion that they
should enter the village together with the outward
appearance of amity, as it would be unwise to let
the warriors have an inkling of the differences that
existed between the white men. Hunt agreed the
more readily because he preferred to have the Spaniard under his eye during his intercourse with these
Indians who were new acquaintances of his but
old customers of his adversary. McLellan saw to
his rifle.

In his speech at the council in the village, Lisa
dissipated in a great measure the suspicions and
ill-feeling against him. He assured the Indians
that, though his party and the Overlanders had
separate interests in trade, he would resent any
wrong done to his rivals as forcibly as if it were
done to himself. He also lent Hunt every assistance in securing horses to convey his men and
baggage overland. Hunt intended to leave the
river at this point and to pursue his way across
the plains, swinging southwesterly through the
country of the Crow Indians and crossing the
Rockies through the Big Horn Range. In this decision he had taken the advice of the three hunters,

Robinson, Hoback, and Rezner, who had urged him to avoid the dangerous territory of the Blackfeet.

Here, then, the Overlanders were to leave the trail of Lewis and Clark and blaze their own path to the sea. It was a foolhardy move; and Lisa might well smile and assist in expediting his rivals on their way to destruction, as he saw it. Had Hunt possessed a knowledge of the wilds and of Indians, he must surely have realized that sixty men, well armed, would have a good fighting chance against raiding parties of Blackfeet, but that sixty men with their mounts and pack horses would be courting disaster in launching into unknown regions where they might lack for game and water and for fodder for their horses. And, indeed, they might expect to lack their horses also, for the Crow Indians were the most skillful horse thieves on the plains. No wonder Lisa was all graciousness. He was to trade horses of his own, pastured among the Mandans, for Hunt's four excellent boats which would probably be carrying the Missouri Fur Company's pelts to St. Louis while the bones of the Astorians lay bleaching on the desert.

On the 18th of July the Overlanders parted with the scientists, who were returning to St. Louis, and set out from the Arikara village with eighty-two horses, pursuing a southwesterly course across the Grand and Moreau rivers. Hunt had not been able to procure mounts for all his people. Most of the horses carried heavy packs containing ammunition, goods for trade, traps, Indian corn, corn meal, condensed soup, dried meat, and other essentials. Hunt and the other partners were on horseback. Dorion and his Sioux mate trudged together, she at his heels leading a horse on which were securely roped the little Dorions and the bundle. An addition made to the party in the Arikara village was a renegade white man named Edward Rose, a sullen creature, of a vicious appearance. Because Rose had lived for some years with the Crows, Hunt engaged him as interpreter.

Towards the end of July the Overlanders, on their southwestern route across the hot plains, fell in with a friendly band of Cheyennes, from whom they purchased thirty-six horses. The bales of baggage were reassorted and one horse was allotted to every two men. After two weeks spent in hunting and trading with the Cheyennes, the cavalcade crossed the Cheyenne River and moved on, now veering south towards the Big Horn Range. On the way, Rose approached some malcontents of the party with a plan to run off the pack horses with their rich bales and join the Crows. These spoils, so he assured them, would win for them high positions in the tribe of his friends. Hunt forestalled the plot by the simple expedient of a bribe, consisting of half a year's pay, a horse, some beaver traps, and merchandise to be given Rose after he had guided the party through the country of his adopted brothers. Thus made sure of his own rise in the world, Rose ceased his altruistic efforts to promote the fortunes of others.

To supply so large a caravan with meat, the hunters ranged afield in small parties. On one occasion three of these hunters missed the trail, and there occurred another agonized separation of the Dorion family, for Pierre was with them. The men had been out for several days, and their comrades had given them up for lost when at last they rode into camp. The stoical look with which the Sioux woman faced her fear through those few days gave way to wild enthusiasm of joy when she saw her heavy-handed lord returning to her safe and sound. The peculiar domesticity of the Dorions Hunt seems to have regarded with a shocked wonder, for on this journey he was making his first acquaintance with the children of the wilderness in their own habitat. Before this time he had known of them only what they chose to reveal across his trading counters in St. Louis.

Hunt's attitude of mind, as well as his material data, was passed on to Washington Irving. We cannot overpay Irving in thanks for the valuable record he made for us from the letters and diaries of the Astorians. But the heart of the life he sought to picture was hidden from him. Hunt and Thorn, men bred in his own world, he understood; but Nor'westers, *voyageurs*, Indians — and the bond between the wild Dorions — were enigmatical to him.

In the furnace heat of mid-August the Overlanders drove on towards the red sandstone crags of the Black Hills, which stretched across the horizon like flames caught and fixed in fantastic outlines by the gods of the mountains. On the heights of that red barrier, said the Indians of the plains, these gods or spirits dwelt. And sometimes they spoke, not only in the thunders they sent hurtling through the sky, but in calm days and even in the silent starry nights when all save gods slept. These reverberations, heard in the Rockies as well as in the Black Hills, have been variously if not yet conclusively explained. Lewis and Clark describe the sound as consisting sometimes of one stroke, sometimes of several loud discharges in quick succession, and resembling closely the sound of a six-pound cannon at a distance of three miles. In some regions of the Yellowstone the sound has a more musical character, suggesting that the gods in those flaming towers have relaxed from wrath to listen while their bards strike upon the strings of a thousand harps.

But whether in wrath or at their pleasures, the gods know well how to guard against any approach to their fortresses of sculptured fire, as the Overlanders, being only mortals, soon learned. Here and there, a corridor would seem to invite them, but it led only to another barred door; and there was little game in these mock passes. Still seeking a way through, they moved southward for several days, and then turned west. Having found their way through the Black Hills, they were now traveling along the ridge which separates the branch waters of the Missouri from those of the Yellowstone; and they were steering their course by the summits of the Big Horn Range far to the west of them. They stumbled upon an Indian trail and followed it for two days into the mountains. Water was scarce and the heat stifling. They saw no more buffalo, for the defiles were bare of grass. Corn meal and a wolf served them for supper one night; and a small stream gladdened their parched throats after twenty-five miles along a waterless route. After another long stretch of hard travel they came out at last upon green sward and water at one of the forks of the Powder River. They took a slow pace up the bank of the river, for buffalo were plentiful here and the hunters were busily killing and drying meat. On the 30th of August they camped near the southern end of the Big Horn Mountains. They had traveled nearly four hundred miles since leaving the Arikara village.

Here they were visited by two scouts from a band of Crows. It was evident that the Indians had kept Hunt's party under observation for some days. Through Rose, the interpreter, amicable relations were established with this band and fresh horses were procured. Then the Overlanders hastened on; they were probably none too certain of keeping the horses they had paid for in goods if the Crows should take a notion to recover them. But the ravines they now entered led nowhere and, after a day of checkmate, they returned to the vicinity of their last encampment. Rose, who had been left with his adopted Crow brethren, came into camp the next morning. He bore a message from the Crow chief inviting the party of white men to accompany his band across the mountains. As Hunt's own attempts to find a pass over the hills had been fruitless, he accepted the chief's offer, albeit with misgivings. So into the narrow mountain trail they went, the Crows leading the way and the white men following. If the Crows were famed for their horse stealing they were no less justly famed for their horsemanship. Every man, woman, and child rode, and their small-hoofed wiry ponies could cling to the face of a cliff and dash along the rocky ledges with the surety of antelopes. Even the two-year-old children rode, strapped with buffalo thongs upon their own ponies. Absaroka, the Bird-People or Sparrowhawks, was the true name of these Indians; but it is said that the French traders, who called them *Les gens des Corbeaux*, and their neighbors on the plains had named them after the prime thief of the bird tribe because, like crows, they flew down from their nests in the mountains, filched whatever took their fancy and bore it aloft where their robbed victims could not follow. However they acquired the appellation, they deserved it. But the name of Sparrowhawk might well have been given them, as a compliment to their riding; for, on their spirited horses, they skimmed through the defiles and over the crests of the ridges like hawks on the wing.

The Crows soon left Hunt's party far behind, but they had shown him the road. Though Hunt had suspected their motives it appears that, for once at least, these mountain magpies had been moved by an honest impulse, for they did not lie in wait for the white men and steal their horses. The next day, the Overlanders met a small party of Shoshones with whom they crossed the second ridge of the Big Horn Mountains and hunted buffalo on the plain below. The Shoshones directed Hunt towards the Wind River, some thirty miles distant, and told him that it would lead him towards the pass which opened upon the south fork of the Columbia River, the Snake; and then went on their separate way.

After journeying up the Wind River for about eighty miles the Overlanders halted to make camp and to take council. In the five days of travel up the river, repeatedly crossing its windings, they had seen no game. Though Robinson, Hoback, and Rezner assured Hunt that, by tracing this river to its source and crossing the one ridge there, he would reach the headwaters of the Snake, Hunt determined to veer again to the southwest where he had heard that another river cut a way through the mountains. There they would again see buffalo. As they reached a high ridge commanding a wide view, one of the hunters pointed to where three snowy peaks pierced the sky far to the west and said that at their feet lay the tributary of the Columbia. These peaks were the famous Three Tetons, first discovered, so far as we know, by the lone trapper, John Colter. In not following the bed of the Wind River towards these grand old pilots, Hunt made another error. The course he took for forty miles, southwesterly along high country touched here and there with snow, led him to the southward flowing waters of the Green River, the north fork of the Colorado. After several days of travel and hunting along its banks, as the river still continued southward, he turned northwest again to seek a pass through the mountains. Eight miles of riding led to a little mountain stream with buffalo feeding about it. Here the Overlanders camped to kill and dry meat enough for the remainder of their journey and to give men and horses a rest. During the eighteen days of September they had crossed two hundred and sixty miles of hard country.

On the 24th of September they broke camp.
Their westerly course across the Gros Ventre Range
led them to a stream where Hoback had trapped
beaver a year before. Hoback's River, as it is
still called, is a tributary of the Snake and therefore one of the source streams of the Columbia.
They followed it through precipitous passes, where
at times there was barely foothold for their horses,
to its confluence with the turbulent and wider
waters of the Snake. Here, in a rugged valley and
within close view of the Three Tetons, they halted.
There was great joy in camp that night. The
evening meal was a feast of celebration; and no
doubt a dance to the scraping of the fiddle and
a shouting chorus were a part of the thank-offer-
ing made by the *voyageurs* and hunters who now
believed that all their troubles were ended.

Near the head of the Snake River, then, the
voyageurs set about canoe-making. As the expedition was now apparently almost within hail of the
Columbia, four of the men who had joined for
the purpose of hunting and trapping cast off from
the party and launched into the wilds. The joy
of the canoe-builders was short-lived. Three men
whom Hunt had sent ahead to explore the river
returned with word that it was not navigable.

Hoback and his two companions now suggested that the party should go on over the intervening ridge, the Snake River Range, to Andrew Henry's fort, on Henry's River, which joined the Snake farther down. On the 4th of October the Overlanders forded the river and began ascending the mountain. On the eighth in a squall of wind and snow they reached the fort. It was deserted.[1] Hunt took possession of the fort for the Pacific Fur Company, turned his horses loose and engaged two Shoshones to take charge of the horses and the fort. Here Hoback, Rezner, Robinson, another hunter named Cass, and Miller, one of the partners, left the party and set forth to hunt and trap.

On the 19th of October the Overlanders embarked on the little river running past the fort, which stood opposite the site of the present Egin, Idaho. Their fleet consisted of fifteen canoes. The stream that bore them presently joined with the waters of the Snake, over six hundred miles above the point where Lewis and Clark had launched their canoes on that river six years before. Down the widened flow sped the canoes, the *voyageurs* singing to the swift rhythmic strokes of their

[1] Henry by this time had reached the Arikara village and rejoined Lisa.

paddles. They made thirty miles before they camped for the night. The next day after twenty miles of easy navigation they began to meet with rapids. In places the men were obliged to make portage along the shore, in others to pass the canoes down stream by the towline. Their dangers and difficulties increased daily. They lost four canoes with most of the cargo in them and the life of one *voyageur*. At length, after some two hundred and fifty miles of water travel, they came to the grand canyon of the Snake where the river, at Shoshone Falls, plunges down through a narrow chasm between towering sides of sheer rock. Several men were sent out to explore. They returned, after having gone forty miles down the river, and reported that the channel continued impassable; the four canoes they had taken with them had been smashed. To add to the gravity of the situation, the party now had only five days' rations.

Here they resolved to separate into four parties. Mackenzie with four men turned northward, hoping that a march across the arid Snake River Plains would bring him ultimately to a navigable branch of the Columbia. McLellan with three men pressed on down along one bank of the Snake and Reed headed a party down the other. Ramsay

Crooks, with six men, went back up the river, hoping to encounter a Shoshone encampment where he might be able to procure food and a few horses. If this hope failed, he would make the long journey back to Henry's Fort and bring the horses for the relief of the main party, which would remain with Hunt at the canyon.

Hunt's men spent three days in caching their goods at the head of the canyon. They caught a few beaver which eked out their scanty food supply. On the third day Crooks and his men reappeared, having realized that the oncoming winter would make it impossible for them to reach Henry's Fort on foot and return through the mountains with the horses, even if they should find the horses still at the fort.

Hunt feared to follow Mackenzie's plan of striking across the lava desert of Snake River Plains because of the lack of water. He decided to keep on down the Snake. He divided his people into two bands. Crooks, with eighteen men, would take the south bank, and Hunt himself, with the same number of men and the Dorion family, the north bank. They set out on the 9th of November, each man carrying his share of the remaining provisions. They had cached most of their baggage, but some blankets, ammunition, traps, and other essentials must be carried. Each man bore twenty pounds, in addition to his personal belongings. Dorion's wife bore her pack, frequently with the added weight of her two-year-old son, while the other child, aged four, marched beside her. There is no record of any complaint from her, although she was now nearing the time when she should give birth to a third child.

Though they followed the river, the high rocky banks made it impossible for them to descend for water, but on the second day they found some rain pools among the rocks. On the third day Hunt and his party reached a camp of Shoshones, from whom they purchased two dogs for their breakfast.

For nearly a month Hunt and his men, with the Sioux woman and her children, wandered through the mountains about the Snake. Sometimes they found a little game or met with Shoshones and obtained a couple of dogs or a few horses. Oftener they hungered. Rain in the gorges and snow and bitter winds on the ridges increased the pain of their travel. On the 6th of December they espied white men coming up the opposite bank. These were Crooks and his companions. Worn with fatigue and emaciated from hunger, they were returning from a point about sixty miles down the river which they could not pass because there were no longer banks and ledges. The shores were mountain walls of rock rising almost perpendicularly from their base in the boiling waters to their crests of snow. Crooks and his party had, perforce, turned back. They had eaten their last meal — their moccasins.

Hunt killed the last horse but one and, hastily making a canoe out of the hide, sent across the river for Crooks. But after Crooks had been ferried across, the canoe was lost, swept away by the current, before food could be taken over to the famished men on the farther bank, and the turbulent waters forbade the employment of a raft. Since Crooks had found the way down the river impassable, Hunt was left with no choice; he also must turn back. Both parties now headed up the river along the opposite banks, retracing slowly their painful steps. Crooks was very ill and could not travel. Hunt remained with him, allowing the others to push on in advance. At length Crooks broke down and could go no farther without food. The one horse remaining belonged to Dorion. He had paid for it with a buffalo robe, and it carried his children and his bundle. He refused to part with it, even for food. Fortunately, before that night they reached a Shoshone encampment and found a number of horses pawing and snuffing for grass under the light snow. Two or three of the hunters crept forward, drove the frightened Indians away, captured five horses, killed one, and set about cooking it. By means of a skin canoe which they made, cooked horse-flesh was now sent across the river to the starving band on the other side. These men had kept heroically on the march, though they had not tasted food for nearly ten days.

The majority of Hunt's men moved on doubling their course up the river they had lately descended. But John Day, who had crossed to Hunt's party from the south side, collapsed. He had been formerly in Crooks's employ in the Sioux country, and Crooks would not leave him now. Hunt was obliged to press on with his party, however, as his leadership and authority were needed, but he left behind with Crooks and Day a *voyageur* named Dubreuil, and two horses and some meat.

On the 15th of December Hunt's party came to a little river, probably Boisé Creek, which they had formerly crossed three weeks earlier. As its banks were inviting, they followed them up some distance and camped in open level country. The weather was so cold that ice was running in the Snake, and snow fell frequently. On the twenty-third, following the lead of three Shoshones from a lodge on the creek who consented to guide them across the mountains, Hunt and his men crossed to the south side of the Snake, near the mouth of another river, probably the Payette or the Weiser. The two parties, now united, moved on together, save for the men left behind, Crooks, Day, and Dubreuil, and three *voyageurs*, who, being unable to march further, asked permission to remain among the Shoshones.

On the morning of the twenty-fourth the travelers turned westward and away from the Snake, but their hardships were not ended. The expedition, consisting now of thirty-two white men, Dorion's wife and children, the three Indian guides, and five horses, made headway slowly and painfully. One sparse meal a day hardly took the edge off their hunger. Rain and snow impeded their march. Heavy night frosts chilled them through as they lay in camp and gave an icy temperature to the streams they were obliged to ford from time to time, as they struck out northwesterly for the chain of forested and snow-covered mountains rising between them and their goal.

In the bleak and snowy dawn of the thirtieth, the Sioux woman began to be in travail; and Hunt, divided between his sense of duty towards the expedition and his feelings of humanity, hesitated about taking up the day's march. Food was very scanty. Every hour of delay was dangerous. Dorion, too, urged him to go on. The party therefore pressed forward, while Dorion and his children remained with the woman. If Hunt cast an anxious look backward at the lonely camp in the wilderness, he may have seen, through the falling snow, the figure of the half-breed bent over the fire close to that dark heap on the ground where his mate contended against the malign powers of cold and starvation for the life bound up in hers.

On the next day the sky cleared. The Overlanders were approaching a Shoshone village south of the Blue Mountains in Oregon. The wintry sun shone on a little valley that stretched out before their gaze, dotted with Shoshone lodges and horses. Here they were hospitably received. On the following day Dorion tramped into the village, leading the skeleton horse which — perhaps with this emergency in mind — he had repeatedly refused to have killed.   On its back sat the Sioux woman with her newborn baby in her arms and her two-year-old boy dangling in a blanket fastened to her body.

It was New Year's Day, 1812, and the men held a celebration.   After a banquet of roast horse-flesh, with boiled roots and entrées of dog and a punch composed of hot water, the musicians of the party produced their fiddles.   The *voyageurs* danced and sang as in the days of their triumphant marches with Alexander Mackenzie, David Thompson, and Simon Fraser of the Nor'westers.   And these tattered and much buffeted men, lean from long hunger and hardship, dropped their troubles with the last sands from the glass of the old year.

For two days the Overlanders rested and fed among the Shoshones.   Then once more they assailed the mountains, where sometimes they sank waist-deep in snow.   By the 7th of January they were descending the farther slope.   The hard travel and the cold had so weakened some of the men that they could not keep up with the main party.   Before that night, the Sioux woman's baby died.   On the next day they came upon another camp of friendly Indians, where they remained until the stragglers overtook them.   Here they procured horses and dogs, and here also they learned that a band of white men had recently gone down the river which flowed by this encampment into the Columbia. From the accounts of the party given him by the Indians, Hunt felt sure that these were the men led by Mackenzie and McLellan. It would seem that this river was the Umatilla which enters the Columbia some distance below the mouth of the Walla Walla. Leaving the river's bank, but keeping a westerly course, the Overlanders reached the Columbia on the 21st of January. Ten days later they were bargaining for canoes with the Indians at the Long Narrows. On the 15th of February the swift tide of the River of the West bore them round the promontory into safe harbor under the shadow of Astoria.

Here they found the men who had set off from the Snake River canyon under Mackenzie, McLellan, and Reed. The three parties had gravitated together in the hills and had forced their way through the canyons of the Seven Devils and Craig Mountains against the terrifying obstacles which had turned Hunt and Crooks back from this route. After twenty-one days of almost superhuman effort, peril, and hunger, they had reached the navigable lower waters of the Snake and followed them into the Columbia. Nothing had been seen by these men of Crooks and Day and the *voyageurs* who had dropped out of the march; and they were now counted as lost.

McDougal and the colony within the fort held a grand celebration in honor of Hunt's arrival. Cannon and small arms were fired, liquor kegs were tapped, and the huge table in the banquet hall was spread with such delicacies as fish, beaver-tails, and roast venison. Fiddles leaped from their bags again on that night and the happy *voyageurs* danced. Well had they earned their right to jig to their heart's content, for, as canoe-men, they had vanquished strange waters, and during six terrible months they had marched with honors over more than two thousand perilous miles.

CHAPTER VI

ASTORIA UNDER THE NOR'WESTERS

THREE immediate tasks faced the Astorians as rainy spring succeeded rainy winter. Dispatches must be sent to Astor, branch trading posts must be established in the interior, and the goods buried in nine caches at the eastern end of the Snake canyon must be recovered.

The loss of the *Tonquin* meant that the letters and reports for Astor must be carried overland. The care of these papers was undertaken by John Reed, and he stowed them away in a bright tin box made specially for the purpose. Reed would make the overland journey to St. Louis in company with Robert McLellan, Ben Jones, a Kentucky hunter, and two *voyageurs*. Two other parties were to set out at the same time — one, under Robert Stuart, to take supplies to his uncle's fort on the Okanogan, and the other, consisting of two clerks, to go to the caches.

Accordingly, towards the end of March, 1812, the three parties launched canoes and ascended the river. Trouble met them at the Long Narrows. The Indians of the village of Wishram above the Narrows, noted for their arts of treachery and piracy, fell upon the canoes. A fight followed; and, before the white men were masters of the field, two Indians had been killed and Reed had been clubbed and wounded and his shining tin box had been stolen. His condition and the loss of the letters canceled the overland expedition for the time being. He and his party kept on to the Okanogan with Robert Stuart and, after some days at the fort there, turned back downstream with the two Stuarts. Not far from the Long Narrows they descried on the bank of the river two naked white men who, on nearer approach, proved to be Ramsay Crooks and John Day. To their old companions it seemed that they had risen from the grave. They had made their way from the Snake canyon through terrible hardship and had recently been stripped of their clothes and moccasins by the Indians at Wishram. The two unfortunates were taken aboard the canoes, fed, and clothed like chiefs in blankets and furs. On the 11th of May they were all back at Astoria.

But the problem still confronted them of how to send dispatches to Astor, and this notwithstanding that they now had a seagoing vessel. Two days before the canoes beached at Astoria, the *Beaver*, Astor's second ship, bearing supplies, was firing inquiring guns off Cape Disappointment. On the eleventh or twelfth a committee of welcome crossed the surfy bar to the ship's anchorage. First went a canoe in which were six Indian paddlers and old Comcomly, who had dressed himself in his best to do the honors. A barge followed propelled by eight *voyageurs* and bearing McDougal and McLellan. Piloted by this delighted reception committee the ship sailed over the bar and came to rest in Baker's Bay. The *Beaver* brought fifteen American laborers and six *voyageurs*, five clerks, including Ross Cox, and a partner named John Clarke, an American who had spent the greater part of his life as a trader in the British Northwest.

The *Beaver*, however, was not available to be sent round the Horn to New York. It was to be used to carry Hunt north to Alaska to bring to fruition Astor's plans with regard to the Russian trade. Astor had broached to the Russian Government his plan for securing to himself and the

Russians all the Pacific coast trade and so squeezing out the free traders. He would furnish the Russians with supplies and ship their furs with his own to Canton. It will be seen that Astor's aim was twofold: to use the coöperation of the Russian traders to drive other rivals off the field and, at the same time, to make the Russian traders dependent upon him — upon his transoceanic and coastwise ships and his colony at Astoria. Hunt was to sail to New Archangel (Sitka) to perfect these arrangements with the Russian official in authority at that port, bring away a cargo of furs, return to Astoria, and transfer to the *Beaver* all the furs collected there, and then dispatch the ship for China.

The reports to Astor could therefore not be sent by sea; it would still be necessary to carry them by land. The duty was undertaken by a party of seven men, headed by the younger Stuart and including Crooks, Day, McLellan, and a *voyageur* named LeClerc. At the same time, Donald Mackenzie and the newly arrived John Clarke, with a number of clerks, *voyageurs*, and hunters, made ready to go inland to seek out good trading sites and erect forts. On the 29th of June both expeditions headed up the Columbia their two barges and ten canoes, while the cannon of Astoria roared a farewell to brave men.

Not far up the river, poor John Day began to show signs of derangement, and Stuart was obliged to send him back to Astoria in care of some Indians passing down on the way to trade at the fort. The parting with his old companion left Ramsay Crooks in great grief. He could not forget his recent experience with Day in the wilderness, when the two men — debilitated from hunger and hard travel and left behind in the barren wilds of the Snake canyon — had sustained and heartened each other, refusing to separate. This is a tale of nobility and loyalty and sacrifice which has never been written. All we have of it is a suggestion. They had no journal in which Day could have set down that the bleak winter sunset found them still in their rocky camp of yesterday and without food because Crooks was too ill to march, and Day himself too weak to range the hills hunting, even if he had dared to leave Crooks alone. And later, when Crooks was able to travel again and Day's wits had wandered beyond the cruel Snake country into the regions of more fantastic fears, there were no means at hand whereby Crooks might record how on such a day he had lost, under a new fall of snow, the tracks of Hunt and his party which he had followed desperately for over a week; or how Indians were hovering among the rocks, surrounding the night's camp but would not draw near either to succor or to slay because of their awe of that supernatural control to which they attributed the ravings of the starved and demented white man.

It is a general belief among savages, and one common among the coast Indians, that madmen are under the control of spirits and are either to be wisely avoided or treated with special consideration and reverence. The Indians bound for Astoria, to whom Stuart and Crooks confided John Day in the last stage of his dementia, guarded him carefully and brought him safely to the fort. Day partially recovered and lived in Oregon for several years only to die in those Snake Mountains, the scene of his sufferings. So came to his end one of the two characters in a lost chapter from the book of Heroism. His name is "writ in water" — but not unto perishing. At least two streams west of the Yellowstone Park are known as "John Day's River," and the place of his death is marked by "Day's Defile."

On the 29th of July the combined parties,

numbering between fifty and sixty men, were trafficking with the Indians on the Walla Walla River for horses. The Walla Walla Indians, of the Chopunnish tribe, were a hospitable and kindly folk and the best equestrians west of the mountains. They owned large bands of horses and they equipped their mounts with crude high saddles after the Mexican fashion. They roamed far afield and are known to have traded with the Spanish in California from an early date, exchanging horses for vermilion and blankets. It was among these Indians, then, that the two expeditions took leave of each other and went on their separate ways.

Nine months later, on April 30, 1813, Robert Stuart and his six men reached St. Louis, accompanied by Miller, the partner who had deserted Hunt on the way out to turn trapper. They had a story to tell of various mishaps, the most serious of which was the theft of their horses by the Crows in the mountains, which forced them to continue on foot so that it became necessary to go into camp for the winter on the bank of the Platte River. In the Snake region Stuart found Miller, Robinson, Rezner, and Hoback — all in hunger and great distress, for they had been robbed of their beaver catch and their guns by Indians. Miller had tasted wild life to his fill and now craved the savors of civilization; but the three hunters asked Stuart for another outfit of guns, traps, and other essentials. These were supplied them from the caches above the Snake canyon, and they pitched their tents again in the wilderness. Only three of the caches were found intact. The other six had been rifled of their contents by Shoshones led thither by the three *voyageurs* who had fallen out of Hunt's starving band and attached themselves to the Shoshones.

The trading caravan, which parted from Stuart at the Walla Walla River, separated into detachments. David Stuart and Alexander Ross proceeded to Stuart's Fort at the mouth of the Okanogan. Here Ross remained while Stuart pushed north up the Okanogan and established another post where now stands the town of Kamloops, British Columbia, at the forks of the Thompson. Far to the east John Clarke built Spokane House at the confluence of Cœur d'Alene and Spokane Rivers. Mackenzie and Ross Cox opened trade with the Chopunnish or Nez Percés from a post which appears to have been on the Clearwater some distance above its confluence with the Snake. Other Astorians went far north up the Columbia to the Pend d'Oreille River, to ply trade with the Salish or Flatheads and the Kootenays, as well as with the "Children of the Sun," or Spokanes, and thus to assist John Clarke of Spokane House in cutting off trade from the posts of the Nor'westers set up on the Spokane and on the Pend d'Oreille rivers by David Thompson the year before. Some of the hunters who went out from Astoria during the winter of 1812 ranged southward into Oregon and are said to have explored five hundred miles inland from the mouth of the Willamette.[1]

Between the winters of 1812 and 1814, the Astorians had spread their trade over an area of country roughly outlined by the Continental Divide on the east, the headwaters of the Willamette on the south, and the Thompson River,[2] New Caledonia (British Columbia) on the north.

But, as will be seen, it was not under Astor's banner that these forts were to flourish.

---

[1] This river is the Multnomah of Lewis and Clark, the Wallámot of Irving, the Willámet and Wylámit of earliest pioneer records. It has sadly strayed from its Indian origin in the silly modern spelling and pronunciation, which mean nothing.

[2] Discovered by Simon Fraser and named by him in honor of Thompson.

13

The Astorians — pushing into unexplored territory in the summer and fall of 1812 — did not know that war had been declared by the United States against Great Britain.   Astor in New York knew it; and his anxiety was great.   The Nor'-westers in Montreal and Fort William knew it; and it was never the way of the Nor'westers to let the water freeze under their keels.   The partners in Montreal and the "winterers" at Fort William, after hearing David Thompson's report on the little colony at Astoria, were resolved to enter at once strongly into contest for trade on the Columbia.   The War of 1812 fell about opportunely for them; it enabled them to color their plans in national and patriotic tints.   War or no war, they would have sent a trading expedition to the mouth of the Columbia to battle by their own methods against the Astorians.   But the war gave them cause to ask a warship of His Majesty.   That would be the swifter way to take the trade — and, with it, Astoria.   So the arrangements were made. Convoyed by the *Raccoon*, the ship *Isaac Todd*, with a group of Nor'westers aboard of her, was to enter the River of the West.   And another expedition was to leave Fort William, paddling and portaging through the maze of waters and mountains from

Lake Superior to the Columbia, and along that great artery to greet the *Isaac Todd* in the bay.

Meanwhile Astor petitioned the American Government for protection for his fort. In response the Government somewhat tardily prepared to send the frigate *Adams* to Astoria, but, at the last moment, canceled the order because her crew was needed to supplement the scanty force on Lake Ontario. And the supply ship which Astor had commissioned to accompany the *Adams* was held in New York harbor by the British blockade. The *Lark*, however, another boat, had sailed with supplies and more traders before the blockade; and Astor could only hope that she would reach Astoria safely and that the men aboard, joining with the Astorians, would be able to hold the fort until the Government could send aid. He may have felt that his hope was a forlorn one, for he remembered, doubtless with misgivings, that McDougal and most of the men at the fort were not only Canadians but old Nor'westers. And Thorn of the lost *Tonquin*, even before war had come to complicate further the already complex ethics of men trained in the Nor'westers' school, had written to him more than once his unfavorable opinion of McDougal's loyalty.

McDougal learned in January, 1813, of the Nor'westers' plans. In that month Donald Mackenzie, just arrived from up the river, brought the word to Astoria. He told how John George McTavish, a Nor'wester trading on the upper Columbia, had dropped in at Spokane House and had confided to both Clarke and Mackenzie what was in the wind. And McTavish had drawn a long bow, as the saying goes; he had spoken of bombardments and wholesale destruction, perhaps also of dungeons for renegade Canadians, and incidentally of a trip he himself meant to make in the spring to contest for the trade at Astoria.

McDougal laid Mackenzie's news before the little group of Astorians and after agitated discussion came to the decision to abandon Astoria in the spring and depart across the mountains for St. Louis. He sent out Mackenzie, Reed, and another clerk named Seton to the forts on the Okanogan, the Pend d'Oreille, and the Spokane, to inform the partners at these interior posts of the intended evacuation, instructing them to bring their furs and goods to the mouth of the Walla Walla, whence they would proceed together to Astoria, protected by their numbers from the pilfering Indians below. They were to trade all their merchandise with the Walla Wallas for horses, keeping only their supply of provisions. Thus provided with sufficient horses to carry the men and the bales of furs that now stocked the warehouses, McDougal planned to make the great hegira of the Astorians on the 1st of July, the earliest moment when they could hope to be ready for departure.

From these instructions it does not yet appear that McDougal was doing any less than his best to safeguard Astor's interests, as well as his own and the interests of the other partners. The plan fell through because David Stuart and Clarke, not liking it, failed to make the necessary purchases of mounts and smoked fish and meat for the journey. McDougal did not become aware of their lack of coöperation until the middle of June, when they finally arrived with their furs. It was then too late to send men back to the Walla Wallas for horses — since Indians are not to be hurried in their trading — and to conclude the necessary preparations in time to cross the high mountains before the descent of winter.

The journey must be abandoned, therefore, until the following year; and what the situation would be then none could foresee. A new peril had been added by the stupid brutality of Clarke and

Farnham, a Vermonter, one of the clerks. These
two men, while among the Nez Percés, had seized
and executed an Indian for stealing a silver cup
from Clarke. The other partners strongly con-
demned the act — this was not the Canadian way
of dealing with Indians — but the mischief was
done. We shall see later how the offended tribe
took their revenge.

To add to McDougal's perplexities, there were
presently visitors at Astoria. Down the river
came John George McTavish of Fort William and
his retinue of *voyageurs* and hunters. It was a
pretty demonstration of the old Nor'wester spirit
that they made, as the fleet of canoes swung into
harbor beside the fort. The men were dressed in
holiday garb — colored fringes dangled from their
caps and shirts, little bells and gay beads clinked
among the fringes of their leggings and sleeves —
and the boatman's songs of Old Canada swelled
from their throats. The brigade went into camp,
while McTavish made himself at home in Astoria
and was given his freedom of the best the fort had
to offer.

McDougal is under suspicion for his reception of
McTavish. Yet it may well appear that the wily
Scotch laird of Astoria was trying to play his game

cannily as possible, seeing that his partners, Stuart and Clarke, by failing to buy horses, had wrecked his best move. There was certainly nothing to be gained by making a foe of McTavish, for the arrival of the *Isaac Todd* and the *Raccoon* might any day make him the Chief Factor of Astoria.

It should be borne in mind, too, that Hunt and the *Beaver* were very long overdue. Unknown to the Astorians, Hunt had changed his plans. Fearing to risk a valuable cargo of sea-otter pelts in crossing the river bar, he had kept on to the Sandwich Islands. He intended to await there the *Lark*, the supply vessel which Astor was to send out, and to return in her to Astoria while the *Beaver* continued her course to Canton. No chronicler has yet doubted the excellence of Hunt's intentions. His motives were always of the best, but the results of his initiative were never fortunate. The belief that Hunt and the *Beaver* had come to disaster influenced not only McDougal; even the obstinate spirit of Stuart was now cast down by it. The upshot of the gloomy deliberations of the partners was that, when McTavish desired to purchase some goods for trade, they sold him not the goods alone but the Spokane trading post. He was to pay in horses to be delivered in the following

spring.   Three of the Astorians then requested and
received of McDougal papers of discharge and en-
rolled with McTavish.   The partners drew up a
statement of conditions, setting forth their rea-
sons for abandoning Astoria and the outlying posts,
and gave it to McTavish to forward for them to
Astor by the winter express which the Nor'westers
sent out annually from Fort William to Montreal.
And on the 5th of July McTavish took leave of the
despondent Astorians and was borne upstream by
his belled and chanting paddlemen.

The partners decided to add to their stock of
furs during the winter, rather than to idle away
the six months before their departure.   Stuart returned to the post at the mouth of the Okanogan
Clarke went to the Pend d'Oreille River; Mackenzie, with a body of hunters, to the Willamette and Reed, with the Dorion family and five
voyageurs including Le Clerc, undertook to trap in
the Snake River country.   McDougal and forty
men remained at Astoria, not a little apprehensive
concerning the tribes in their immediate vicinity.   It was in this summer month of July, 1813
that McDougal, having exhausted all other means
of terrorism and diplomacy, offered himself — a
more or less willing sacrifice — for the safety of

the Astorians and became Comcomly's son-in-
law. And exactly one month later, to the very
date, his spouse's brother burst into the bridal
bower with news of a ship in the offing. There was
great excitement within the fort. Was it the *Isaac
Todd?* Or the *Beaver* returned after a year away,
like a ghost from Neptune's realm? Was it His
Majesty's ship *Raccoon* with guns to batter down
the fort? Nearer came the ship and now the
watchers could see the Stars and Stripes at her
masthead. Shouting with joy, they rushed to the
guns and fired a salute. McDougal was already
rowing out in a small boat to meet the vessel.
As twilight closed in the boat returned and Mc-
Dougal and Hunt sprang ashore. The ship was
the *Albatross*, chartered by Hunt for two thousand
dollars at the Sandwich Islands, after he had
waited in vain for months the coming of Astor's
supply ship, the *Lark*, which, unknown to him,
had been wrecked.

Though Hunt was greatly perturbed at the idea
of abandoning Astor's vast schemes for the Pacific
coast trade, he finally agreed to the decision which
the other partners had made. His first concern
was in regard to the furs. He resolved to sail in
the *Albatross*, which was bound to the Marquesas

and the Sandwich Islands. He hoped to charter a vessel at the latter port in which to call for the furs and carry them to market in Canton. It was agreed that if he did not return, McDougal should make whatever arrangements he could with McTavish. Hunt confidently expected, however, to be back at Astoria by the 1st of January. Even so he would have been too late to have a voice as to the disposition of Astor's property, but as a matter of fact he did not return to the Columbia until the 28th of February.

On the 7th of October, about six weeks after Hunt's departure, John George McTavish with a brigade of seventy-five men in ten canoes were again wafted down the river to the jingle of bells and the music of boatmen's songs. He knew that the *Isaac Todd* and the attendant warship must be nearing Astoria and he intended to beat them there. The two Astorians, Mackenzie and Clarke accompanied the brigade. They had fallen in with McTavish up the river while on their way to the upper posts and had turned back in the hope that they might succeed in gliding down ahead of him and so get the news to McDougal and plan their moves before the Nor'wester's arrival. But their chance never came to leave that Nor'wester behind in the night. McTavish had given orders to his men to sleep with one eye open and an ear to the ground: The two Astorians did slip their canoes noiselessly into the stream one morning before dawn, but only to see, in the first light, two other canoes full abreast of them; and, with what cordiality they could muster, they said "Good morning" to McTavish.

Irving, taking a long-distance view, alleges that McDougal might have dictated his own terms, because the Nor'westers were out of provisions and had lost their ammunition; that he might, in fact, have made off up the river with the furs. Be that as it may, McDougal now surrendered Astoria to the Nor'westers and sold them, under agreement duly executed, Astor's stock of furs and goods and the buildings and boats, and all the forts on the Columbia and the Thompson at about a third of their value. Thus the rapacious Nor'-westers had turned the trick not only against their rival, John Jacob Astor, but also against the British Government. A month later, when His Majesty's ship the *Raccoon* sailed into the river, it only remained to hoist the British flag above Astoria and to rechristen the captured post Fort George. There is no record saying that the

privilege of performing these loyal ceremonies was
considered by His Majesty's officers as full com-
pensation for the loss of the rich prize in furs,
which they had made all speed to capture, having
been egged on thereto daily by a Nor'wester they
had aboard, John MacDonald of Garth. The
feelings of the naval men, indeed, were such that
they held no pleasant teas or banquets on board
the *Raccoon* in honor of McDougal or MacDonald
or McTavish. And, if McDougal's canny, un-
warriorlike conduct so grieved His Majesty's bluff
and simple mariners, what was the effect upon
another heart in Astoria? Poor old Comcomly!
Having witnessed the bloodless surrender of the
fort, the great chief retreated to his lodge, hid his
face and his one eye under his blanket and mourned
that his peerless daughter — she of the proudest
lineage and the flattest head among the Chinooks —
should have married not a man but a squaw.

When Hunt returned in February to find Astor's
property disposed of and the Union Jack waving
in place of the Stars and Stripes, there, too, was
McDougal, now acting as Chief Factor of the
Nor'westers' post of Fort George. The dissolu-
tion of Astor's company, as provided for by con-
tract, had left him free to rejoin the Canadians.

There remained nothing for Hunt to do but to receive the drafts on the North-West Company for the sum of the bargain price and arrange about forwarding them to Astor by a small party of Astorians headed by David Stuart, Clarke, and Mackenzie, who refused to join the Nor'westers and who were about to cross the mountains. Hunt then reëmbarked.[1]

In April of that year (1814) the *Isaac Todd* arrived. The ship brought several distinguished lights of the North-West Company, among them an autocratic old gentleman named Donald Mc-Tavish, whose rôle was that of governor of the new domain, but whose chief aim in life was to keep a full goblet beside him, an aim rendered difficult by the continuous motion he made for emptying it. To assist him in solving his problem, old Donald had enlisted the services of a barmaid named Jane Barnes, whose Hebe-like skill and swiftness in pouring had won his heart in an English alehouse. This barmaid was the first white woman on the Columbia. Her flaxen curls, blue eyes, and ruddy cheeks so inflamed the heart of Comcomly's son that he offered one hundred sea-otter skins for

---

[1] Hunt returned to St. Louis and in 1822 was appointed Post-master by President Monroe.

the privilege of marrying her; but the Governor would not surrender his fair one. Let us hope that the old Governor quaffed at least one of his many cups nightly to the bold adventuring spirit which had made young Jane Barnes shake the dust of a sailor's alehouse from her bare feet and dare the high seas and the savage wilds

> For to admire and for to see,
> For to be'old this world so wide.

A little longer than thirty days did Governor McTavish hold high revels. The journal of the younger Alexander Henry, who came to Astoria with one of the Nor'westers' canoe brigades, tells how high ran the tides of rum within and about Fort George. From other sources we learn that in June those tides came into conflict, so to speak, with the swollen flood of the Columbia, when a canoe bearing the Governor, Alexander Henry, and half a dozen *voyageurs*, all rather more than less unbalanced by their liquor, was overturned, and the Governor and Henry were drowned. When her patron sank inappropriately into a watery grave, what became of venturesome Jane? History seems to be mute. But there is a rumor to the effect that she sailed away to China and captured the heart of a magnate of the East India Company, who built a palace for her.

In July of the previous year, it will be recalled, a party of seven men, with Pierre Dorion and his wife and children, had gone into the Snake River country under John Reed's leadership to trap. There Robinson, Hoback, and Rezner had joined them. When David Stuart, Clarke, Mackenzie, and their party of Astorians set out from Fort George on April 4, 1814, to cross the mountains, they expected to find Reed and his band, inform them of the changes that had occurred, and take them across country to St. Louis, if they should desire to go east rather than enlist with the Nor'-westers. The latter choice was open to them, because it was a part of the agreement between McDougal and McTavish that the North-West Company should endeavor to find places for any of Astor's men who might wish to remain in the territory.

As Stuart and his companions neared the mouth of the Walla Walla they heard a voice hailing them in French. They turned in towards the bank. It was Dorion's wife calling to them. She had a tragic story to tell. In the winter she had gone

along the Clearwater with Pierre, Rezner, and Le-
Clerc to a beaver stream. It was in the Nez
Percés territory, a five-days' journey from Reed's
post. While she was at her work of dressing
skins in the hut one evening, LeClerc entered
bleeding from wounds. Indians had fallen upon
the three men suddenly and LeClerc alone had
escaped alive — barely alive, for he collapsed as
his tale was told. The Sioux woman quickly
caught two of their horses, loaded her children and
some food on one of them and, after binding up
LeClerc's wounds as best she could, lifted and
roped him upon the back of the other. Leading
the horses she set off swiftly into the dark winter
night towards Reed's trading post. Three days
later as her keen eyes searched the landscape, she
caught sight of a band of mounted Indians riding
towards the east. She lifted LeClerc down and hid
him with herself and her children and the horses.
That night, a cold January night, she dared not
make a fire. She snuggled her children in her
garments to keep them warm but the cold was too
severe upon LeClerc, weakened from wounds; and,
when morning came, he was dead. On the next
day, when the Sioux woman reached Reed's encampment, she found only the horrible traces of

slaughter. She fled towards the mountains where the Walla Walla cuts its way from Idaho into Washington; and there she camped in a ravine under a shelter of skins and cedar branches until spring, subsisting meagerly on the smoked flesh of her horses. When milder weather came, her food was nearly gone. She started out again with her children, crossed the mountain and went down along the river bank until she arrived among the hospitable Walla Wallas, who took her in and cared for her and her children.

The woman could give Stuart no reason for the massacre nor say by what tribe it had been committed. But, as Clarke heard her tale, perhaps his mind reverted to the scene he had staged nearly a year before in the vicinity of these murders. And, if so, he saw now with different eyes the gibbet of oars erected on the spring grass by the beaver stream and the Indian, who had been tempted to theft — like a child or a magpie — by a brightly gleaming cup, bound and slung in the noose and strangled while his tribesmen looked on with expressionless faces till his struggles were over and then took up his body and silently went on their way.

So was savagely snapped the savage bond which

had held Pierre and his Sioux mate together
through harsh seasons within their tents and
through hunger, cold, and the hourly peril of death
in the wilderness. The last picture we have of
Dorion's wife is as a fugitive among the Walla
Wallas, telling her story to Stuart.   But ten years
later there was a young Indian named Baptiste in
the brigades of the Hudson's Bay Company in
Oregon, who was the eldest son of Pierre Dorion
and the Sioux woman.

CHAPTER VII

THE KING OF OLD OREGON

THE war with Great Britain came to a close with the Treaty of Ghent in December, 1814. It was a peace without victory, and all captured territory, places, and possessions were to be restored to their former sovereignty. Astoria was not mentioned in the treaty, but in negotiations immediately subsequent a demand for its return was made by the United States. The British Government demurred on the ground that Astoria was not captured territory, since the valley of the Columbia was "considered as forming a part of His Majesty's dominions." Eventually, by a liberal construction of the term "possessions," Astoria, built by an American, was restored to the United States, but the question of the ownership of Oregon was left open.

Neither nation at that time had any real sense of the value of Oregon nor anything but the vaguest idea of its possible boundaries. Great

Britain did not then, or later, herself lay sovereign claim to the whole region. Her attitude was less aggressive than defensive; she desired to protect the British traders in their rights. Since the question of title had been mooted, in 1818 a convention provided that the two nations should jointly occupy the country for ten years. So began the Oregon dispute, which in course of time led perilously close to a third war with Great Britain.

Before the Joint Occupation Treaty of 1818, some effort was made by John Jacob Astor and his friends to have the *status quo ante bellum* clause in the Treaty of Ghent construed to cover his lost property at Astoria; but his arguments could hardly be convincing when it was disclosed that the North-West Company had paid — however inadequately — for everything received. Astor's heavy losses on the Columbia and at Michilimackinac through the war made him feel bitter. He never forgave McDougal for having sold his furs to the Nor'westers because, if the furs had been seized, he could have recovered their value under the treaty. The American Government could not collect salvage for John Jacob Astor, but it could assist him in another way. At his instigation Congress passed a law forbidding alien traders to operate within the bounds of the United States except as *engagés* of Americans. This law was enacted in April, 1816. It served to keep British traders out of the territory about the Missouri and off the southern shores of the Great Lakes, but it could not, of course, touch the Nor'westers in their operations beyond the mountains. They still occupied Astor's forts by right of purchase. So the curfew knell which Astor had sounded for their especial benefit rang for the most part unheeded. No doubt it was discussed ironically at the suppers in the Beaver Club of Montreal when Astor appeared in that town to buy furs.

Astor was willing, even anxious, to send out more traders and ships to the Pacific Coast and to begin his daring scheme all over again. He had a spirit nothing could daunt, and his dream was worth any cost and all effort. But he realized that without support from his Government he could not hope to drive the Nor'westers from Oregon. Had he been granted his request for one military post on the Columbia with fifty soldiers and the rank of lieutenant for himself, he would have proceeded, even by arms, if need be, to make John Jacob Astor the master of the world's fur trade. But the American Government was not minded to take any step contrary to the spirit of the treaty just entered into with England. The war, and the international agreements resulting from it, had made Astor's dream impossible of fulfillment. His affliction, however, was proportionately less than that of his partners and employees, if life be reckoned above money. In the massacre of the *Tonquin's* crew, in the wreck of the *Lark*, in the loss of life among the Overlanders by hardship and Indian wrath, not less than sixty-five men had perished. The partners, including McDougal, received nothing for their two years of toil and peril in the wilderness.

With his Pacific Fur Company dissolved and the business of his Southwest Company — his partnership with the Nor'westers in the Mackinaw trade — suspended by the war, Astor was obliged to confine his activities to his American Fur Company. To establish a western department at St. Louis, from which to send out his own traders into the fur country of the Missouri and Yellowstone rivers, was his immediate necessity if he wished to survive as a fur merchant. Here was Astor hoisted by his own petard. The Nor'westers, at their rollicking suppers, might well jest at the statute of 1816 which Astor had instigated against them; for the

Missouri Government, influenced by the St. Louis traders, used that statute to bar Astor from St. Louis and to permit the seizure of his goods and furs on the river on the pretext that, as British traders chiefly formed the personnel of his company, his business was unlawful. It was not until 1822 that he finally secured a foothold in St. Louis.

Meanwhile the Nor'westers, having got themselves into a sea of trouble, were obliged to strike their colors. Their piratical activities in the North had stabbed fully awake the drowsy old Hudson's Bay Company. The old Company had suffered many outrages from its rival. Not only were its brigades robbed on the march, but some of its trading posts were attacked, its furs and supplies carried off, and its servants wounded or killed by the lawless Nor'westers.

It was in 1811 that Lord Selkirk, a Scotch nobleman, purchased shares in the Hudson's Bay Company and acquired a vast tract of that Company's lands as a preliminary step in his scheme to found a colony on the Red River. In August, 1812, the first colonists arrived and set up their huts on the site of the present city of Winnipeg. The colony was soon beset by the Nor'westers. Failing to discourage the settlers by peaceable means, they resorted to violence, which culminated in 1816, in the killing of the Governor of the colony and twenty settlers. Finally Lord Selkirk himself, armed with powers as a Justice of the Peace, and accompanied by a number of disbanded soldiers who desired to take up land, set out from Montreal to the Red River. He escaped the Nor'westers' hired assassins lying in wait for him, made a number of arrests at Fort William, and he sent the culprits east for trial. Thus it came about that John Jacob Astor, buying furs at the North-West Company's depots in Montreal, had the satisfaction of seeing in the clutches of the law some of the dare-devil gentry who had thwarted him.

The riotous conduct of the Nor'westers and its results were made the subject of parliamentary inquiry in Great Britain in 1819; and two years later the North-West Company was absorbed by the Hudson's Bay Company. It was a victory for Law and Order. The Nor'westers were strong men and they had done great things in the wilderness. Their Alexander Mackenzie had followed to the Arctic Ocean the great river which bears his name, and he was the first Anglo-Saxon explorer to cross North America overland to the Pacific. Their Simon Fraser had discovered the Fraser

River and passed down its roaring waters almost to the sea. Their David Thompson was the pioneer explorer of the whole Northwest and of the Columbia River from its source to its junction with the Snake. Through such men as these, and through violent, hardy men who knew no virtue save courage, had they conquered the wilds. But even in the wilds they could not defy the law. Beating against that rock, their company lost its existence.

So it was that the old Hudson's Bay Company, the ancient "Company of the Adventurers of England," established law and order in the Oregon country and raised over the forts built by the Astorians and appropriated by the Nor'westers the old banner with the letters H. B. C. in its center.

Hither, to Robert Gray's river, came to rule the man who is now known as the Father of Oregon or the King of Old Oregon. John McLoughlin was of Irish and Scotch blood and a Canadian by birth. He was born in 1784 in the parish of Rivière du Loup far down on the St. Lawrence River. For a time he practised medicine in Montreal. Later he went to Fort William as resident physician, developed an interest in the trade, and joined the Nor'westers as a wintering partner. He was not of the same quality as the roisterers who gathered at Fort William. The uprightness of his character, the distinction of his bearing, and his dignified and kindly manner would have found fitter place from the first in the service of the Hudson's Bay Company.

It was as an officer of the Hudson's Bay Company that John McLoughlin was to come into his own and to make for himself a name imperishable in the annals of Oregon. He was not quite forty when he arrived on the Columbia, a man of striking appearance, about six feet four inches in height, broad-shouldered — a commanding figure. His piercing glance, overhanging brows, and broad forehead swept by a plume of white hair, won for him the title of "White Eagle" from the Indians. His official rank was Chief Factor, but his subordinates called him "Governor."

This man was to rule for twenty years as the autocratic monarch of the Pacific Northwest. It was a régime of equity in trade and of personal morals. McLoughlin took to wife the Indian widow of Alexander Mackay, who perished on the *Tonquin*, and adopted Mackay's children. He set the example of marital fidelity and compelled every man in his employ who had taken an Indian wife to conduct himself as if State and Church had

united them for life. He was, indeed, State and
Church in Oregon. His moral force dominated
white men and Indians alike.

In 1825 McLoughlin abandoned Fort George, or
Astoria, and made his headquarters at his new Fort
Vancouver, up the river about six miles north of
the mouth of the Willamette. Fort Vancouver
was an imposing structure, as befitted the Capitol
of a primitive realm. It was built in the shape of
a parallelogram. Its dimensions were 750 by 500
feet, and it was enclosed in a stockade of closely
fitted timbers twenty feet high. Within the walls
the space was divided into two courts with a number of wooden buildings facing on them. There
was a powder magazine built of stone. McLoughlin's house stood in the center of the enclosure facing the huge gates. It was a large two-storied
mansion of logs containing, besides the private
rooms for himself and his family, an imposing dining room, a general smoking room, and a visitors'
hall. Some of these rooms were decorated with
mounted elks' heads, skins, Indian cedar blankets
and baskets, and other ornaments contributed by
admiring natives. In the court, at each side of
the mansion's doors, stood two cannon with piles
of balls. Below the fort on the edge of the river

stretched a growing village of cabins. Here lived
the married laborers, servants, *voyageurs*, and hunters; and here also, in time, were built a hospi-
tal, a boathouse, a storehouse for cured salmon,
barns, a mill, and a granary and dairy house.

Cultivation of the land from the fort to the river
was begun at once, and gradually a farm extended
on all sides and along the Columbia, about nine
square miles in all. McLoughlin realized that the
forts west of the mountains must be supplied with
foodstuffs from some point within their own territory, as the cost, the risk, and the delay occasioned
by the transportation of food by land and by sea
from the eastern coast were too great. Accordingly, besides planting grain and vegetables, he imported a few cattle from California as soon as a
vessel could be procured in which to bring them
north. In time the King of Old Oregon could look
from the upper rooms of his mansion over fifteen
hundred cultivated acres and beyond to a grassy
prairie where roamed more than a thousand cattle.
There were dairy farms on the mainland and on
Wapato Island in the mouth of the Willamette;
on this island were the dairy buildings from which
products were shipped north to the Russian posts.
On the south side of the Columbia where the

Willamette empties itself there also gradually rose
a few rough dwellings, spreading southward along
the banks of the smaller stream. These were set
up principally by *voyageurs* whose years of fighting
white water were done. McLoughlin encouraged
the old servants of the company to farm. Whatever these small farms produced above their owners'
needs found a ready market among their neighbors
and the Indians.

This was the real beginning of settlement in Old
Oregon, out of which the States of Oregon, Washington, and Idaho, and part of Montana, were afterwards carved. The story of this farthest "West"
is a romance of the fur trade. The "Wests" between the Appalachians and the Rockies were first
settled by bold and restless men who went into
the wilderness and battled with the Indians for
land. The fur trader truly had been there before
them, for he was always the first man to enter the
Indian's country, but he had founded no settlements. In Old Oregon, however, settlement was
begun before ever a white-covered wagon crossed
the plains. The beginning of Oregon City was in
the first cabins raised and the first garden patches
planted by old servants of the Hudson's Bay Company. Settlers seeking homes, of the same kind as

those who reared villages in Kentucky and Missouri and Ohio, were to come later; but, when they came, they were to find a wilderness already yielding to the plough. They were to see neat cabins, arranged so as to outline narrow streets, and patches of planted grain, and to hear the tinkle of the dairy farm and the whir of gristmills and sawmills. Here, only, the fur trader did not pass with the beaver and the deer, leaving the land and the forest untouched. Even in the story of its first settlements, then, Old Oregon is still the romance of the fur trade. And it was John McLoughlin's idea — the planting of these tiny hamlets and farms where the aged *voyageurs* and hunters might settle down to safe and useful living, instead of being cast forth as human driftwood when their best days as brigade men were past.

McLoughlin's chief lieutenant was a young man whom he had brought from Fort William with him "Black Douglas" was the sobriquet bestowed on this tall handsome youth with the dark skin and raven hair. James Douglas, afterwards prominent in British Columbia, was, like his chief, a Highlander born far from Bonnie Scotland. It was in Demerara, British Guiana, in 1803, that Douglas first saw the light. At twelve or fifteen years of age he accompanied an elder brother to Montreal, where he presently became an apprentice in the North-West Company.

Another man in McLoughlin's ranks was Peter Skene Ogden, brigade leader and explorer. Ogden also had been a Nor'wester; and, like McLoughlin, he was born in Quebec. He was a rather short, rotund man with a high voice and a merry round face. He always had a jest for any one who would listen and was inordinately fond of practical jokes — characteristics which made him a striking contrast to his two dignified friends, Douglas and McLoughlin.

From Fort Vancouver McLoughlin sent out his brigades east, north, and south, and directed them to set up new trading posts. He sent Douglas to Fort St. James, on Stuart Lake in New Caledonia; and forts were erected throughout that northern territory as far as the Stikine and Taku Rivers. It was a far cry from these northern outposts to another erected about the same time on the Umpqua River in southwestern Oregon. Centrally situated in the interior on the Colville River, arose Fort Colville. This was an important post, a sort of clearing house or bookkeeping headquarters for the accounts of the whole country. The clerks from the lesser posts brought their accounts to Fort Colville to be audited and transcribed for the annual report which was sent across country by the annual express brigade to Norway House on Lake Winnipeg.

From Fort Vancouver went out all the supplies for the northern forts west of the mountains. The route followed to the interior posts, roughly speaking, was by canoe and barge up the Columbia to Fort Okanogan, thence by horse to Kamloops Lake, then by water again down the Thompson River into the Fraser to supply Fort Langley near the mouth of the Fraser. To reach the northern posts in New Caledonia the brigades usually took to horse at Kamloops and rode the two hundred odd miles up the Fraser to Alexandria, where again they dipped upon the surface of that river and poled and towed upstream about 150 miles to Fort George at the mouth of the Nechaco, thence by the Nechaco River to the fort on Stuart Lake. The earliest brigades traversed more of the way by water, with sometimes long and hazardous portages.

Southward, the brigades under Ogden or Tom Mackay went into California. And eastward Ogden led his men beyond Salt Lake. He was

presumably the first white man to see Mount
Shasta and the headwaters of Sacramento River.
He discovered the Humboldt River. He penetrated
into the desert of Nevada. He explored Idaho, a
part of Utah, and tracked through the rugged
country between the Snake and the Colorado.

In the Rockies and east of them Ogden's brigades met and clashed with the men of the American Fur Company — in which now, as partners,
were Ramsay Crooks, John Clarke, and Robert
Stuart — and with General Ashley's men from
St. Louis, or the Rocky Mountain Traders, as they
were called. Manuel Lisa was dead and the Missouri Fur Company was bankrupt; but Lisa's partner, Andrew Henry, had formed a new company
with Ashley. The Rocky Mountain men paid the
Indians double the Hudson's Bay Company's prices
for furs and, defying the laws of their Government,
they opened a fountain of rum in the wilderness in
their effort to starve Ogden off the ground. They
lay in wait for the H. B. C. brigades, or set the Indians on to attack them, and pirated their furs. It
was war to the knife. The Blackfeet and Shoshones,
profiting by the lessons thus inculcated in them, developed a fine impartiality towards all white traders and robbed all alike. One year they stole 180

beaver traps from Ashley's men. Ogden had his revenge, too, when some St. Louis traders were caught by snow in the hills. The Indians, under his influence, refused to make snowshoes for them until Ogden had bought at his own price the furs which they had hoped to market in St. Louis.

The use of liquor gave the St. Louis traders a large advantage over the H. B. C. men, for McLoughlin prohibited rum as an article of trade; but ultimately they suffered for it at the hands of the Indians to whom they had taught the vice of drunkenness. The Rocky Mountain Traders and the American Fur Company fought each other as bitterly as they fought the Hudson's Bay Company. Twice, at least, Rocky Mountain Traders who had been pilfered by rivals or Indians staggered, stripped and starving, into H. B. C. forts and asked for succor. McLoughlin's men received the unfortunates hospitably. They sent one man safely home to the Mandan country under escort. In the other case they dispatched a brigade to recover the furs and to lay down the law to the thieving tribe. Though they did not let the trader take out the furs, they paid him for them the market price and sent him also safely on his way.

It has been urged by some writers that the

Indians were stirred up to violence by the Hudson's Bay Company, not only in their attacks on traders but later in the massacre of American settlers in Oregon. That charge is well answered by the facts concerning settlement and trade in New Caledonia and Rupert's Land (now Canada), where, under the Company's rule continued for two centuries, trade was carried on and, later, settlement took place without a single massacre initiated by Indians. In Oregon, McLoughlin carried out the policy of the Company, which had a fixed price for furs and which meted out the same justice to an Indian as to a white man. If a white man had exhibited an Indian scalp in Old Oregon he would have been tried formally and hanged.

The fur brigades which went out east, north, and south from McLoughlin's rude castle on the great river were small armies under tried captains. A brigade would consist of fifteen or twenty-five white men, fifty or more Canadian, Indian, or half-breed trappers, and enough horses to supply each man with three. It was McLoughlin's policy to send the wives and families on the march with the men. The women cooked and dressed skins in the camps; and their presence acted as a deterrent to those wilder spirits among the men who would have met war with war but for this responsibility. To the tribes the presence of women was always a sign of peaceful intent. The northern brigades bound for the upper Fraser set off in spring by water. Canoes and barges were launched upon the river to the singing of the *voyageurs*. The horse brigades for the south and east took the trail in autumn. A bugle called the men into line on the day of the march, and Highland pipers played them off. "King" McLoughlin, in his long black coat and his white choker, with his white eagle plume floating in the breeze and his gold-headed cane in his hand, stood in the gates to give them Godspeed. In every brigade there were fiddlers, and sometimes a Scot with his bagpipes went along to rouse the men in a black hour with *The Cock o' the North.*

Frequently McLoughlin and his wife rode out at the head of the Willamette brigades. The King's presence was dearly coveted by the men, and Mrs. McLoughlin delighted in these excursions which broke the monotony of life under a fixed roof. The lady of Fort Vancouver sat upon a gaily caparisoned steed with bits of silver and strings of bells clinking along her bridle reins and fringing her skirts. Her garments were fashioned

of the brightest colored cloths from the bales at the
fort and she wore "a smile which might cause to
blush and hang its head the broadest, warmest and
most fragrant sunflower," while at her side, also
handsomely arrayed, "rode her lord, King of the
Columbia, and every inch a king, attended by a
train of trappers under a chief trader each upon his
best behaviour."

In addition to the H. B. C. trade by land, there
swiftly grew up on the Pacific an overseas and
coastwise trade. The overseas trade was chiefly
with China. On the coast, vessels plied between
Fort Vancouver and San Francisco, where the
Company had a trading post, and between Fort
Vancouver and the Russian posts in Alaska.
These ships also carried supplies to the Company's
forts on the northern coast. The Russian Fur
Company did not like the proximity of British
posts, and it induced the Russian Government
to rescind the right of other than Russian vessels to navigate Russian streams. The Russian
territory was held to extend farther south than
McLoughlin's Fort Simpson on the Nass River,
just north of the present Prince Rupert. The
dispute ended, as far as the H. B. C. was concerned, in the lease by the Company of a strip

of the Alaskan coast, lying between Cape Spencer and Fort Simpson, for a rental of two thousand sea-otter skins yearly.

In this year (1839) the H. B. C. had a fleet of not less than half a dozen vessels sailing at regular seasons from Fort Vancouver. Among these was the *Beaver*, the first steamer on the Pacific coast. The *Beaver* had left London in 1835 as a sailing ship, rounded the Horn, and dropped anchor before Fort Vancouver in 1836. Here she was fitted out with machinery and became a steamboat. The *Beaver* lived to a ripe old age in the coast trade and was wrecked at last in the narrows at the entrance to Burrard Inlet. There, until a few years ago, the hulk lay impaled on the rocks below Stanley Park and could be seen by passengers on the great ocean liners entering and leaving the harbor of Vancouver, British Columbia.

McLoughlin urged his company to purchase the whole of Alaska from Russia. And, as the spirit of revolt blazed up in California, he pointed out the ease and advantage of acquiring that country also. He sent his son-in-law, Glen Rae, to San Francisco with funds and with instructions as to how to gamble in revolutions for the advantage of the H. B. C. This plan met with disaster when Glen

Rae met with a certain beautiful Carmencita and forgot all else. That is one of the stories. The other is that Rae picked as winner, among several revolutionary factions, the one which was doomed to be last under the wire. He achieved nothing but the loss of the Company's funds, and he shot himself rather than return and tell the whole truth to the "King" in Oregon.

But whether his plans went well or ill, Mc-Loughlin did not lose the serenity in which his power was rooted. Not the whole strength of the Hudson's Bay Company could have made Mc-Loughlin a king whose rule was unquestioned if his had not been a kingly spirit. Men who had brawled and roistered and known not the name of law under the Nor'westers' régime now stepped softly.

The daily life of the King and his courtiers and his motley subjects in the feudal realm of Old Oregon is worth a passing glance. There is nothing like it in the United States today, nor was there ever anything like it during the pioneer days in other parts of the country. Nowhere else on American soil have white men gone in numbers of a hundred or more with a train of employees and built forts and houses, tilled fields, set up mills, and herded cattle in the midst of the red man's country, to be received by the natives not only as friends but as rulers.

The keynote of life at Fort Vancouver was work. On the Sabbath, men rested — and worshiped; but there was no idling on week days. A huge bell, mounted in the court on three poles and sheltered from rain by a small slanting roof, rang at five in the morning to rouse officers, clerks, and laborers to the day's duties. At eight it called them in from the fur houses, mills, and fields to breakfast, and at nine rang them out again to their toil. At noon it sounded for dinner, and an hour later for work again. At six o'clock it announced the evening meal and the end of the day's labor. The King rose with his subjects, for McLoughlin kept an active supervision over the various operations at headquarters. He was also for some years the only physician in Oregon, and many were the demands upon his skill, for men who had been out in the sleet and cold of the hills or in the long rains of the coast winter frequently came home with rheumatic pains and fevers.

We are inclined to think of the life in that farthest West as a barren life for a man of intellect and culture such as McLoughlin. But that view is erroneous. McLoughlin's chief officers were men of his own stamp. He himself had studied his profession of medicine in Paris and had spent some time in Great Britain; and among his comrades in Oregon were university men from Oxford and Edinburgh. Books and conversations on serious topics, such as history and international relations, in which subjects these men were well versed, were their relaxation. The brigades from Hudson Bay and sailing ships brought the London *Times*, however late, and also volumes of history, biography, travel, and agriculture. The classics could be found on the shelves in the living room of the Big House and the modern poets were there, as well as the novels of Lord Selkirk's friend, Walter Scott. From time to time the ships brought distinguished visitors from the Old World, and sometimes such visitors came overland. A few of these were men of science, like Nuttall who had first ventured into the wilds with Lisa's brigade, and David Douglas, the Scotch botanist whose name was given to the northwestern fir tree. Globe-trotters and big game hunters of that day also came to Fort Vancouver. All guests were warmly welcomed to King McLoughlin's rude castle for as many weeks or months as they chose to remain, and horses and servants for their personal use were assigned to them.

McLoughlin's chief interest apart from trade was agriculture. He had engaged a scientific Scotch horticulturist named Bruce, who was making experiments with both indigenous and imported plants. Bruce coaxed the wild strawberry plant to produce a large luscious berry and the wild rose to expand its blossoms. His apple trees, grown from seed, flourished. He failed, however, to persuade the Californian fig and lemon trees to endure the Oregon winters. King McLoughlin took the greatest interest in these experiments, and in the growing season hardly a day would pass without a visit to the frames and beds where Bruce was matching his science against the climate and the habits of wild plant life.

Another point of interest in the establishment was the large smithy where tools and machinery were repaired and where hatchets and axes for trade, as well as for the use of the fort's laborers, were made.

If in imagination, on a tranquil summer evening, we stand with the King of Old Oregon on the bank of the River of the West, we may read there the

prophecy of Oregon's future destiny in the world
of modern commerce. From the little sawmill
comes the hum of the saw and the drumlike sound
of green timber planks dropping upon the wharf, for
the Company's bark lying at anchor will carry
a cargo of lumber to the Sandwich Islands. So
we have a tiny glimpse of the beginning of the
vast timber trade of the north Pacific coast. Far
down, the river is black-dotted with long high-
prowed cedar canoes, and the air blowing up
stream brings a sound of many voices in chorus.
It is a sound too shrill for melody, but the wild,
piercing "oh-ah we-ah!" has in it something in
keeping with the blood-hued flare across the western sky and with the drench of colored light which
envelops the river and tips the somber forest with
fire. The Indians are singing their Song of the
Catch, as they float down to the bay to fish. In
their canoes are spears with bone hooks — and
some with iron hooks now, since the opening of
the smithy — and nets woven of cedar and grass
fibers. They will drop their weighted nets, stretching each net between two canoes, and some of the
men in both canoes will hold an end of the net
while the other men paddle. In this fashion they
will sweep the waters and snare the salmon that

rush thickly into the river. The first fish caught will be offered in thanksgiving to the Creator of all things. After this ceremony has been performed the other salmon will be split and boned and hung up to dry in sun and smoke on racks erected along the shore and on the rafters and roofs of the houses. When winter draws near, the dried fish will be marketed to the tribes of the interior. Thus, primitively, these Indian fishers and barterers forecast the salmon trade which, in the future, shall contribute so large a part of the wealth of Oregon. The tinkle of bells as cows are driven up to the milking, the young fields of grain and vegetables, and the little spirals of smoke above the cabins announce that this is a country of yielding earth, a pleasant land for homes. These farms and cabins, planted at McLoughlin's behest, not only forecast the acres of grain fields and apple orchards, the stock ranches and the hamlets and cities of homes which constitute the Oregon of our day, but they mark the beginning of the end of Old Oregon and its King. In the coming democracy of the soil his feudal kingdom is to pass away.

As the King reënters his castle, the great bell tolls the end of a day's work. Officers, guests, clerks, brigade leaders, gather in the huge dining room.

The autumn brigades have not yet departed, so some forty men sit at the tables tonight; and there are enormous roasts to feed them.

In the group immediately about McLoughlin are James Douglas, Ogden, Tom Mackay, the Payette whose name endures in Idaho, Nuttall the botanist perhaps, or a British army officer on leave, and maybe an American trader who has fought the fur battle unsuccessfully in the mountains and has been forced to throw himself upon McLoughlin's mercy, such as Nathaniel J. Wyeth, with whose little band Nuttall crossed the Rockies. A piper stationed behind the King's chair plays while hungry men, bronzed and hardy from a life in the open, make amends to their stomachs for lean days in the desert lands and for supperless nights when they tightened their belts and lay under their blankets in the snow-choked passes. The memory of famine gives zest to the dinners at the Big House. Between courses Ogden, with twinkling eyes, cracks his jokes. Then Tom Mackay, the irrepressible story-teller whose Indian blood shows in the imagery blended with his humorously bragging recitals of the games he has played with death beyond the mountains, begins a tale with his invariable formula: "It rained, it rained! it blew, it blew! and my God how it did snow!" And McLoughlin, pouring the one small glass of wine which he allows himself, laughs. He laughs as a King may who knows not one traitor nor poltroon in all his realm. If this is the evening of his reign, there is a glow upon it warmer than the red of sunset and kindled by a spirit stronger than wine.

As we conjure up the scene of the evening meal in the Big House, we are reminded of illustrations we have seen in books about medieval Scottish life. The huge room with its two wide stone fireplaces, its bare timbered walls and log rafters, and following the line of the walls, its long tables weighted with steaming platters where twoscore men feast by candlelight, seems to be the replica of the banquet hall in the rude castle of some Highland chieftain in the days of Bruce. Here, too, we easily distinguish the chief, for his demeanor bespeaks the man who earns his right to command by his deeds. And, when we consider the points of likeness which the clan system and the primitive code of the Scotch Highlanders bear to the tribal system and code of the red men, we can understand how it was that the Highland factors and brigade leaders of the great fur companies triumphed over their rivals and held the friendship of the Indians.   Each brigade was as a separate division of the clan under a petty chief; and all these chiefs were subject to the head of the clan.   The Indians understood this system because their own confederacies were formed on much the same plan.   With them, also, the chief must prove his right by his deeds — by good deeds or evil deeds, if so be that they were strong deeds. The American traders they regarded only as traders and as friends or foes, according to their mood.   But the Scots were chiefs of tribes, after the fashion of Indian chiefs.

The man who sits at the center of the banquet table in the Big House, with two tall candles lighting up the platter of roast venison before him and the kilted piper standing behind his chair, is not only Chief Factor John McLoughlin, head of the white clans in the western division.   He is Chief White Eagle, head of the tribes; and in the gossip, story-telling, and song which enhance the feast of venison and salmon in the red men's huge lodges this night, White Eagle's name and strong deeds, his eye and word of command, and his great stature, are the favorite themes.   Honorable and mighty are the tribes who have White Eagle for their chief!

CHAPTER VIII

THE FALL OF THE FUR KINGDOM

IT was in 1832 that Nathaniel J. Wyeth, of Boston, crossed the plains to give McLoughlin battle on Oregon soil. Wyeth duplicated Astor's plan of campaign. He sent out a ship with goods for trade and with provisions; and he himself at the head of a small party of men set off by land. For various causes several of his men left him on the way, and fortune did not smile with unwonted benignity on the remainder, nor on the enterprise in general. Wyeth and a few of his party reached Fort Vancouver in need. The ship was wrecked. McLoughlin received the tattered wanderers hospitably and let them have whatever they required from the stores of the Company in exchange for labor or on credit.

When Wyeth returned to Boston it was to plan another expedition. He sent out the ship *May Dacre* to meet him at the mouth of the Columbia, and he once more proceeded to cross the continent,

accompanied by a band of young New England-
ers whom his accounts of El Dorado beyond the
Rockies had fired with enthusiasm.   This time
Wyeth's ship put into port safely, and he had
goods and men enough to warrant him in establishing two posts for trade.   He built one post on
the island in the mouth of the Willamette and
erected Fort Hall, his headquarters, on the Snake.
McLoughlin then sent Payette to build Fort Boisé
near Fort Hall in Idaho, and the Indians passed
Wyeth's fort by and took their trade to the post of
the Company, whose personnel and methods they
knew and trusted.   Nor would they come to his
Willamette post.   Wyeth, defeated, sold out to
McLoughlin and returned to New England, where
he prospered in other branches of commerce.   His
venture as a fur trader scarcely caused a ripple on
the surface of life in Oregon, but in the East it
kindled interest in the territory beyond the mountains, an interest dormant since the days of Lewis
and Clark.   Was Oregon a land for settlement?
Men began to ask that question.

But Wyeth's excursion while it had some effect,
was not the chief cause which led to settlement.
To the Salish Indians — wrongly named the Flatheads, because this tribe did not practice distortion

16

— belongs the honor of having awakened the East on the subject of Oregon. In 1832, the year of Wyeth's first venture in Oregon, two old men and two young warriors of the Salish journeyed from Flathead Lake in the mountains through the dangerous country of their Indian foes to St. Louis, to seek out William Clark and to request from him a Bible and a holy man to teach their tribe what was in that book. The Salish had closely observed the Hudson's Bay Company's traders in Oregon and had concluded that it was something in the trader's Bible which made the white man a man of power. From the *voyageurs* they had heard of priests who instructed the ignorant in the ways of righteousness; they had heard, too, through other tribesmen of the "Black Robes," for the tradition of these great missionaries of New France was a part of Indian lore[1]; and being themselves,

[1] Of all early missionaries to the North American Indians the French Jesuits have left the most illustrious name. Members of the Order first arrived at Quebec in 1625. They came thereafter in great numbers and dwelt among the Indians everywhere as far west as the Mississippi and as far north as Hudson Bay. After the fall of New France (1760) an edict of the British conquerors forbade the Jesuits to add to their numbers in Canada, but permitted those already in the country to remain and "die where they are." The last priest of those who remained died in 1800. An American reprint of their *Relations*, edited by R. G. Thwaites, was published in seventy-three volumes (Cleveland, 1896–1901).

nephew Daniel Lee, two missionaries of that de-
nomination. By McLoughlin's advice the Lees
settled in the growing settlement on the Willamette and not in the territory of the Salish.
No doubt missionaries were less needed by the
Salish than in the spreading village and farming
community peopled by the old *voyageurs* and laborers of the Company and also by some sixty white
settlers who had straggled into Oregon from various parts. These settlers had married Indian
wives and were bringing up a flock of children
without religious counsel of any sort. McLoughlin had already provided them with a school-
teacher named Solomon Smith, a Harvard man of
Wyeth's first band, who took root in the country
by marrying Celiast, daughter of the Clatsop chief,
and began a family and farm of his own.

In 1835 the American Board of Commissioners
for Foreign Missions sent out the Reverend Samuel
Parker and Dr. Marcus Whitman to found missions among the Indians of Oregon. By this date
steamers were plying on the Missouri River, but
the steamer which bore these missionaries got
the worst of an argument with snags or sand bars
and so came to a halt at Liberty, Missouri.
From this point the missionaries and the party

of traders under whose escort they were to proceed to Oregon took horse and pushed overland through the valley of the Platte, following that route first made by the buffalo, then appropriated by the Indians and the fur traders, and now known to history as the Oregon Trail.[1]

At one of their encampments in that country of the Teton Range — lying between the headwaters of the Platte and Green rivers on the east and the headwaters of the Snake on the west, where Astor's Overlanders wandered long and helplessly, and where later Ogden's brigades clashed with the traders of St. Louis — Parker and Whitman met bands of Salish and Nez Percés. These Indians evinced so keen a desire for religious instruction that Whitman decided to turn back with an east-going brigade and bring more missionaries. Parker continued the journey over the mountains, guided by a party of the eager Salish. These Indians, says Parker — who kept a journal — "are very kind to each other, and if one meets with any disaster, the others will wait and assist him." They had not proceeded far when they met a large

[1] Father de Smet says that the Indians called this trail, marked deep by the wagon wheels of the settlers, the "Great Medicine Road of the Whites."

band of Nez Percés coming to greet the holy man, advancing in columns, the warriors leading and the women and children in the rear — all singing for joy, while their drummers beat out the rhythm of the march.

Although provisions were scarce and it was dangerous to delay, Parker pitched camp so that he might impart spiritual food to the several hundred primitive souls who thus sought him in the wilderness. He preached to them a number of sermons. They can have understood very little if anything of what he said, but he preached from the Bible, and so they knew that his words must be true and mighty; and they were happy. A buffalo hunt followed, and Parker was presented with a large quantity of cured meat and twenty buffalo tongues. A hundred and fifty Indians remained with him and brought him to the Hudson's Bay Company's post at the mouth of the Walla Walla. Here they left him and returned over the mountains to rejoin their hunters. The officer at the post sent Parker down the river to Fort Vancouver, where McLoughlin made him welcome.

Parker visited the site of Astoria and the tribes about the mouth of the river and saw for himself why McLoughlin had quitted Astoria and had moved his trading headquarters sixty miles up the Columbia. He found the Chinooks besotted and degraded with liquor from the trading vessels which put into Baker's Bay from time to time. Before the founding of Astoria the Chinooks, under the stern governance of Comcomly, were sober Indians. It is even recorded that the old chief once strongly reprimanded his son-in-law, McDougal, for giving rum to Comcomly's son, causing him to return drunken to the Chinook village and to make a shameful spectacle of himself before his tribesmen. But during the reign of the Nor'westers, it seems that the Indians lived in a state of debauch, continued since then by means of liquor from the American trading vessels.

In the following spring Parker traveled through the valley of the Walla Walla, the Snake, and the Spokane rivers, noting favorable sites for missions, and late in the year (1836) he set sail from Fort Vancouver. After an absence of two years he returned to his home, at Ithaca, New York, and immediately published his *Journal of an Exploring Tour Beyond the Rocky Mountains*. This made another wind to fan the rising interest of easterners concerning Oregon.

The Macedonian cry from the Salish country

was not disregarded by the King of Old Oregon. If the savages themselves were petitioning for a teacher of the Scriptures, it began to appear that the white men in Oregon should also make request. McLoughlin wrote to his superiors in London asking for a chaplain to be sent to Fort Vancouver without delay.   In due course a minister of the Church of England arrived, accompanied by his wife.   This lady was the second white woman on the Columbia and, as chance would have it, her name also was Jane and her last initial B.   The name of this couple in fact was Beaver — a circumstance which was merrily hailed as a good omen among the fur traders, since beaver was the standard coin of the fur realm.   But, alas, Jane Beaver was as inappropriate in her way to wilderness life as ever Jane Barnes had been.   Mrs. Beaver refused to associate in any way with the Chief Factor's wife, or with the wives of his officers; and Beaver himself publicly denounced McLoughlin and Douglas for the iniquity of marriages legalized only by the common law of the wilderness.

Douglas's wife, Nelia Connolly, the daughter of a white man, was able to understand the words that were unintelligible to the Cree wife of McLoughlin, and the scorn and condemnation of the

Englishwoman bewildered her and struck her with grief. Douglas, in temperament the opposite of his chief, cold, cutting, and doubly punctilious in anger, conveyed his impressions of the Reverend Mr. Beaver to that gentleman and insisted on the immediate performance of the marriage ceremony. Not so McLoughlin. That insulted monarch flew into a rage and drubbed the over-zealous moralist from the fort with his gold-headed cane. And, refusing to consider any rite performed by Beaver a sacred one, he would not submit to a ceremony at his hands but peremptorily ordered Douglas, lately equipped with powers as a Justice of the Peace, to unite him legally to the mother of his children.

McLoughlin, when his fury had passed, made public apology for his action with the cane, fearing that he had done what might diminish the clergyman's possible influence for good in the community. But Beaver found himself unable to accept the apology, and as soon as possible he and his lady sailed away from that jungle of iniquity — and ferocity. They had contrived, with the best intentions, to do no small harm during their brief visit. Ritualism and convention had met with the primal and the self-lawed, and the test had been too severe for both.

Misunderstanding was mutual and perfect. The Beavers, from their sheltered English parish, where conduct was ordered in advance and where no greater danger threatened them than being caught out in the rain without their galoshes, could not even guess at the nature of the feelings they had stirred and outraged in the husbands of the Indian women at Fort Vancouver. If they had known how to listen, they could have heard from those husbands tales of feminine heroism which might have enlightened them, tales of how death from some wrath of Nature or from human foe had missed its mark at the man only because of the woman's spontaneous reaction to her creed which declared her own life to be nothing outside his service. Ogden has recorded two occasions when the Salish woman saved his life and one gallant episode when she sprang to horse, pursued the party of rival traders and Indians who had seized his furs, dashed into the caravan, cut out the pack horses and stampeded them back to her husband's camp under the leveled rifles of his foes. And sixteen-year-old Nelia Connolly had leaped to the place of danger before her young husband, as hostile Indians rushed upon him in the lonely northernmost fort in New Caledonia. Such memories as these gave fire to the fury of the King; for was it not he who had issued the ukase that, if any man dealt unfaithfully by an Indian woman, he could not remain in the service of the Company or in Oregon?

In 1836 Marcus Whitman and his bride, accompanied by Henry Spalding and his wife and W. H. Gray, a lay helper, arrived at Fort Vancouver. Mrs. Whitman and Mrs. Spalding were the first white women to cross the continent to Oregon.[1] The missionaries had come by covered wagon from Fort Laramie to Fort Boisé, where Payette had put them in the charge of Tom Mackay's brigade, then about to start homewards. They were received with enthusiasm and every offer of service was made to them by white men and Indians alike, so that their passage from Boisé to Walla Walla and down the Columbia was like a triumphal procession. Word had been sent ahead to McLoughlin, and, when the Whitmans and Spaldings landed, they found the King and his court on the bank to welcome them.

On McLoughlin's advice, Whitman went to the Cayuse Indians about five miles west of Walla

[1] Ten years earlier Manuel Lisa's wife had crossed the plains with her husband to his fort at the mouth of the Big Horn.

Walla, and Spalding established himself at Lapwai on the Clearwater among the Nez Percés.   While waiting for their new dwellings to be made ready for them, the two young women remained in the Big House and undertook to give instruction to McLoughlin's children.

In 1838 McLoughlin went to London to confer with his superiors.   From all signs, as he read them, the Treaty of Joint Occupation would soon cease to operate.   By the terms of this treaty, signed in 1818, Great Britain and the United States had agreed that the subjects of both governments should have equal rights within the territory west of the Rockies for ten years.   The treaty left the question of title to this region in abeyance.   Ten years later the time was extended indefinitely, with a clause providing that the agreement could be terminated by either party on twelve months' notice.   A second decade had now run its course, and there was little disposition on either side to continue the agreement much longer.   In the notes exchanged by the two Governments prior to 1828, the United States had expressed a willingness to consider an adjustment of the boundary at the forty-ninth parallel all the way to the Pacific. But the British Government, pointing out that this line would cut off the southern end of Vancouver Island, would not consent and presently suggested that the line should be drawn down through the middle of the Columbia River, leaving the navigation of that stream free to both parties. This suggestion the United States rejected.

The workings of diplomacy were watched closely by the officials of the Hudson's Bay Company in England, and very probably those officials made suggestions to the British Government. At all events, they seem to have thought it likely that the Columbia would ultimately be decided upon as the boundary, for Fort Vancouver was built on the north bank of the river and the brigade leaders who ranged south of the river were instructed not to conserve the game but to follow up all the beaver streams, and, in short, to trap out this part of the country. Early during his reign at Fort Vancouver, McLoughlin became convinced that the country south of the Columbia, today the State of Oregon, would soon attract settlers, and that, whatever the diplomats might decide, the territory would belong in the end to the nation which colonized it. It was with these several thoughts in his mind that he sent the old servants of the Company into the Willamette Valley to settle. There settlement could not interfere with the fur trade and, later, it might hold the territory for Great Britain. McLoughlin wished to see all the western country from Mexico to the Arctic Ocean under his nation's flag.

But now the Americans were coming in; and, if they settled the country, the same principle would apply in their case. So far he had been unable to induce the Company's officers in London to undertake colonization in Oregon as they had done on the Red River in Rupert's Land. Sir George Simpson, the Governor of the Hudson's Bay Company, ridiculed the idea that Oregon would ever be a Mecca of overland migration. He thought the difficulties too great and also that Oregon was not a farming country. But the old King knew better. Therefore he went to England to declare his views in person before the directors of the Company and to plead for action.

His visit was not successful. The Company did, indeed, agree to send out a few men to farm under the grant of a new company to be formed and to be called the Puget Sound Agricultural Company; but they made light of his prognostications in general and rather let him feel that he was taking too much upon himself in giving advice.

McLoughlin reached home towards the end of 1839. Immediately he was confronted by a new problem created by the influx of missionaries and one which he could now do little toward solving. In the year before, Jason Lee had gone east for more helpers and had returned by ship bringing with him more missionaries and their families and some settlers. It had been McLoughlin's policy to advise each missionary to seek a separate field where his activities would not overlap those of any other religious teacher. Creeds were unimportant to him, as indeed they were to the other sons of the wilderness. And because it was not creeds but knowledge of God and the Commandments which mattered to man, he had, five years since, appointed Jason Lee, the Methodist, to the settlement of French-Canadian Catholics on the Willamette, for as yet no priest of their own Church had entered Oregon. There Jason Lee performed marriages and baptized children. Whitman and Spalding, McLoughlin had sent to different tribes, so that each tribe should have but one white leader of light and thus should not be confused by a divided authority. But the missionaries, some with their families, who had come on Jason Lee's ship were settling wherever the soil looked most promising for wheat. Moreover, two Catholic missionaries, Blanchet and Demers, had arrived from the Red River and had begun their labors on the Willamette and at Fort Walla among Whitman's Cayuses. Father Pierre Jean de Smet, a Belgian Jesuit from St. Louis, came in 1840 and settled among the Salish. Other priests quickly followed and toured the Indian territory, preaching and baptizing; and there were presently in Oregon about sixty missionaries, itinerant and stationary. More settlers came and also some American traders. The latter were not attached to the American fur companies but were small peddlers; and the chief article of trade on their pack horses was liquor. When the brigade leaders came in next spring (1840) they reported to McLoughlin that the Indians were uneasy because so many people were coming in, and were already sorry for their invitation to the missionaries.

Because of later happenings, it is worth while to understand the Indian point of view. With the Indians of the North Pacific territory, who lived either on the seashore or along the larger rivers inland, water was not uncommonly used in some of their religious rites, because chiefly on the waters and by the products of the waters they lived. Therefore they took very kindly to the rite

17

of baptism.   When Protestant and Catholic missionaries wrote in their diaries that they had baptized scores of eager Indians daily, they were not exaggerating.   For when the Indians learned that near by there was a white holy man who could perform a Strong Magic with water, they traveled in droves to partake of the blessing.   So far so good. But presently they were told that the baptism they had received so happily was impotent to save them.   According to Indian logic that meant a bad magic, and it might harm them very much — by bringing about a fish famine, for instance.   Thus did they interpret the white man's dispute of creeds; and dissensions arose among themselves as to the respective merits of the missionaries.   And each year they saw more white men coming in and taking up their land, for which they were paid nothing.   They began to be very suspicious as to the true purpose of the white holy man's magic. Add to these perplexed questionings the incitement of the free trader's whiskey, and we have the fundamental causes of the Cayuse War which was to break forth within a decade.   Tragedy was inevitable, although most of the men and women who taught the Gospel in Oregon were devoted spirits, willing not only to live their lives among the

Indians but to *give* their lives for the creeds they taught and for the salvation of their red-skinned brothers.

McLoughlin now was between two fires — his Company's displeasure and the animus of the new settlers. Sir George Simpson came out in 1841 and, on looking over the books of the Company at Fort Vancouver, was furious because of the credit given to the Americans. McLoughlin retorted that he would not allow these men to starve. What most stirred Simpson's anger probably was the proof before his eyes, in the tents and cabins, that McLoughlin's prophecies of settlement — which he had scouted — had been true ones. On the other hand the settlers and even some of the missionaries, whom McLoughlin had received kindly and had generously helped, distrusted him. They did not understand the old King and his sway over Oregon. Two eras of civilization, historically more than a hundred years apart, were touching and clashing in Oregon — the eras of old feudalism and of modern republicanism. Those who so readily vilified McLoughlin and the Hudson's Bay Company did not know that, during these few years, only the old King's fiat held the Indians back from slaughter. They did not know that a native deputation had waited upon McLoughlin and requested permission to wipe out the strangers who were speaking evil words against him — nor that these red-skinned deputies had been driven from Fort Vancouver in disgrace, with the threat of ostracism from the Company's trade and from all its benefits if they lifted a finger against the newcomers.

In 1843 Marcus Whitman, returning to Oregon from a visit to the East in connection with the affairs of the mission, fell in on the way with a caravan of over nine hundred settlers and guided them across the mountains. The men were accompanied by their wives and families and all their worldly goods. The Great Migration into Oregon had begun.

Winter caught the caravan in the mountains. Through snow and sleet the immigrants straggled to the bank of the Columbia. Here they built rafts to float them down. And on one of these rafts, as it shot through the Dalles under the pelting of rain, a baby was born. It was night and stormy with wind and rain when the first of the fleet neared Fort Vancouver. McLoughlin ordered his men at the fort to turn out to aid the rain-soaked pilgrims in mooring the rafts and in landing the household goods. Bales of blankets were carried down. All night the clerks over their books made entries of supplies sent out by a small army of runners. McLoughlin ordered the women and children taken to the Big House, where his wife ministered to their needs. He remained on the shore till morning in the driving rain, directing the work of his men. His presence meant more than the settlers guessed. It was a sign to the Indians. The explanation, which he wrote to his superiors in London, of the large accounts carried on his books for the settlers and missionaries will bear recording here. It was to the effect that, if he had shut the gates of the fort and the doors of the storehouses against the immigrants, the Indians would have fallen upon them and the charge would have been made by those who were jealous of the Company's preëminence that its officials had set the natives on to murder these people.

The growth of the American population made it necessary now for the settlers to organize a provisional government, since they were unwilling to acknowledge the authority of McLoughlin and the Hudson's Bay Company. The first convention of Americans met in 1843,[1] at Champoeg on

[1] As early as 1838 settlers had petitioned Congress to establish a territorial government for their protection; and on several occasions throughout 1841 and 1842 public meetings had discussed the advisability of setting up a provisional government.

the Willamette near the present Salem, Marion
County, and chose three commissioners to govern
them.   Two years later they framed a constitution and appointed a governor.   The new government was opposed by the British settlers and by
Douglas.   But McLoughlin supported it and contributed to its first exchequer.   The missionaries
living among the Indians were not in favor of it,
for the deposing of McLoughlin meant that there
was now no authority which the Indians would
recognize.   The natives were becoming more sullen and resentful daily because of the great con-
course of white settlers; and there was now no check
at all upon whiskey peddling.

Meanwhile the Oregon Question was convulsing
Congress and a part of the nation on the eastern
side of the mountains.   A year before the Oregon
settlers appointed their governor and subscribed
to a constitution, President Polk had been swept
into the White House by the slogan of "Fifty-four
Forty or Fight," which meant that Great Britain
must recognize as American soil the whole Pacific
coast from the northern boundary of California
to the southern limits of Russian Alaska — 54°
40′ — or else the United States would declare war.
Negotiations were in progress between John C.

Calhoun, Secretary of State, and Richard Pakenham, on behalf of the British Government, when Polk declared, in his inaugural address, that "our title to the country of the Oregon is 'clear and unquestionable.'"[1] Yet, in spite of these statements and the loud response they evoked, Pakenham made two proposals to submit the question to arbitration; but both were declined by Buchanan, the new Secretary of State, who said uncompromisingly that the United States would arbitrate no question involving its territorial rights.

But by the spring of 1846 the United States was at war with Mexico. To fight Great Britain at the same time was impracticable. Though there was furious recrimination in certain quarters in England, as the echo of the bloodthirsty speeches of Congressmen and Senators sounded across the Atlantic, the British Government marked out for itself a course, described by Lord Aberdeen as "consistent with justice, reason, moderation, and common sense." On June 6, 1846, Pakenham sub-

[1] When Polk in his annual message amazed his followers by stating that he had continued the negotiations begun by Calhoun and had offered to compromise on the forty-ninth parallel, it was recalled that he had not repeated the phrase of the Democratic platform — "the *whole* of the territory of Oregon." This offer of compromise was not accepted by Great Britain and was subsequently withdrawn.

mitted to Buchanan the draft of a treaty which was signed six days later without amendment or alteration. The President sent the treaty to the Senate for consideration without his signature. This was a reversal of the usual procedure; but the overwhelming majority in favor of signing the treaty (37 to 12) in a degree at least saved Polk from the appearance of a wanton change of front.

By the terms of this treaty the boundary line between the territories of the United States and those of Great Britain was continued westward along the forty-ninth parallel to the middle of the channel which separates Vancouver Island from the mainland; thence it proceeded southerly to Juan de Fuca Strait and through the center of that strait to the ocean, thus securing the whole of Vancouver Island to England. Navigation of the channel and strait was to be free and open to both signatories; and navigation of the Columbia River was to be free to the Hudson's Bay Company and to those trading with them; and the possessory rights of the Company and of all British subjects in the territory were to be respected.

This settlement was eminently just. It gave to the United States the territory rightly claimed through Gray's discovery of the Columbia, through

Lewis and Clark's descent of the lower part of the river, and through the planting of Astoria. On these facts the American right to the Columbia Valley rested soundly. The United States had also, in 1819, acquired Spain's claim to the coast, through the treaty which ceded the Floridas and all Spanish territory on the Pacific north of California. But the Spanish title to Oregon was a shadowy one. Spanish mariners had done no more than land on the coast and declare possession; and, two hundred years before they did so, the Englishman Drake had sailed along the north Pacific coast and had taken possession of "New Albion" for his sovereign.

Great Britain's claim to the Northwest Coast — Oregon, Washington, New Caledonia, and Vancouver Island — was based on the explorations of Cook and Vancouver, on Mackenzie's overland journey to the sea, and on the explorations and establishments of the fur traders. The British right to New Caledonia (British Columbia) and Vancouver Island is easily seen to be indisputable now that the mists of controversy have evaporated. Indeed, even when the argument was raging, Calhoun advanced England's right in conversations with Polk, as Polk's diary reveals, and more than once urged upon Polk's attention the fact that England could claim the country watered by the Fraser by the same right that the United States claimed the country watered by the Columbia, pointing out that the Hudson's Bay Company had built a score of trading posts on the Fraser and its tributaries and had begun colonization at Victoria on Vancouver Island.

The Oregon Treaty gave to both the United States and Canada a broad outlet on the Pacific, with the opportunity to expand their settlements to its shores and their commerce across its waters.

Unfortunately the lurid and acrimonious language of many Congressmen and Senators was reflected by the populace — now about ten thousand — in Oregon itself. There was discord between the Americans and the British and unreasoning animosity against the Hudson's Bay Company and its officials and servants. This unfriendly feeling began as early as 1841. Lieutenant Wilkes of the United States Navy, visiting Oregon in that year, commented on the attitude of the settlers towards the Company which had treated them with such great generosity, and expressed his surprise. There is no doubt, however, that the Company's servants, whose regard for

McLoughlin was little short of adoration, resented the intrusion of the settlers and their new government, and contributed their share of strife. Those were the blind days when jingoism ranked as patriotism, and when a man's love for his own flag was measured largely by the hatred he felt for his neighbor's. Ill-will did not prevail with all, but it did prevail with too many. It was finally to pass away in the exercise of democratic government and in blood, when the Indians rose against the white dwellers in Oregon and thus accelerated their union.

In the year of the Oregon Treaty, McLoughlin resigned from the Hudson's Bay Company and retired with his family to Oregon City. He was succeeded by Douglas at Fort Vancouver. The Indians took the departure of "White Eagle" from the Big House bitterly to heart, and they blamed the Americans for this stroke of sorrow. McLoughlin knew that as a deposed chief his power was broken; he could no longer command the natives. He sent word up the river to the Whitmans and begged them to come into the settlement, but they would not leave their post among the Cayuse Indians.

A few months later an epidemic of measles broke

out and a number of sick were being nursed at the
Mission House by the Whitmans and their helpers.
The disease spread among the Indians, and Whitman and Spalding had their hands full. The natives were terror-stricken. Some of them, at least,
believed that the white people had purposely let
loose this scourge to wipe out the Indians. No
doubt they had heard of Duncan McDougal and
his corked bottle of smallpox and concluded that
the missionaries could have kept the bottle of
measles corked if they had half tried. The epidemic seems to have been the spark which touched
off the stored-up fears and resentments of the
Indians. The wanton murder of numbers of their
red kindred just beyond the hills by Bonneville
and other American adventurers, the seizure of
their lands by settlers, whose first great caravan
these Indians had seen enter their country under
Whitman's guidance, were other causes of their
sullen discontent.

The Whitman mission was attacked. The
Whitmans and twelve others in it were murdered.
Some fifty persons were taken away as prisoners.
The government of Oregon, powerless to effect
the rescue of the captives, appealed to Douglas.
Ogden with some of the men of his brigade followed

the Indians into the mountains and induced them to surrender the prisoners.

When the Indian risings began, the Hudson's Bay Company stopped the sale of firearms to the natives. But the insane prejudice abiding in the minds of some of the settlers and missionaries inspired a few of Oregon's early chroniclers to set down the cause of the uprising to the machinations of the Company.[1] Some of the farm lands belonging to the Puget Sound Agricultural Company were seized by settlers in defiance of the Treaty of 1846, and attempts were made to wrest McLoughlin's holdings from him. But the Father of Oregon had many friends as well as foes among the settlers, and these stood by him loyally.

John McLoughlin died in 1857, aged seventy-three. A few years before his retirement from office he had turned for comfort, in the storms of

[1] Not only the Company but the Roman Catholic priests were accused; and a storm of Protestant and Catholic recrimination rocked Oregon. The histories written by W. H. Gray, a Protestant layman, and Father F. N. Blanchet show how far men of zeal but of narrow sympathies may be led to forget the injunction that "he who hateth his brother is a murderer." Marcus Whitman was a Christian in his life as well as in his death. Father de Smet's devoted labors among the Salish reveal the Catholic missionary at his highest. Even those men who dipped their pens in gall had not hesitated to stake their lives in pursuit of their ideals. The Indian war would have come in any case.

censure and prejudice that broke over him, to the Canadian priests who had come into Oregon, and he died a devout Catholic. His latter years saw no change in his large spirit of tolerance and good-will towards loyalties and faiths other than his own. In soul and mind, as well as in bodily stature, McLoughlin towered high above most of the men of his day in Old Oregon. He got little gratitude in his lifetime and for years after his death, a cloud rested upon his memory. But the pages of scurrility about him have been faded white by the light of the truth, and his name and fame are today treasured as a great tradition in Oregon. He was a master builder, for he erected the moral structure of law and of just and humane principles in the wilderness; and it was under the shelter of his building that settlement began and grew in peace for a decade.

The Indian outbreaks which began in 1847 and continued for a generation compelled the American Government to provide for the security of the settlements, and, in 1848, the American domain west of the Rockies was erected into Oregon Territory. In 1853 it was divided and Washington Territory was set up. Six years later, on February 14, 1859, the State of Oregon was admitted to the Union with its present boundaries.

So passes Old Oregon.   So dawns the new régime.
Great changes have come to that country west
of the mountains in the thirty-five years since
McLoughlin went to live there! Portland, first
settled in 1845, is now a chartered city and the
home of Oregon's first newspaper, the *Oregonian*.
There is a settlement at Seattle, named after a chief
who remained friendly during the Indian wars. Victoria, on Vancouver Island, whither Douglas moved
the Pacific headquarters of the Hudson's Bay Company in 1849, is a thriving colony.   The capital of
McLoughlin's feudal kingdom, Fort Vancouver, is
the county seat of the new Washington Territory.

The Hudson's Bay Company will shortly sell to
the United States Government all its property
on the American side of the boundary.   The old
Company is now no longer a feudal overlord but
only a trading corporation. Its domains to the
north, west of the mountains, have been surrendered to the Crown and two new colonies, Vancouver Island and British Columbia, which are
presently to become one, are beginning their history. James Douglas is the Governor of both
colonies. A few years more and these colonies,
together with the fur trader's vast northern empire of Rupert's Land and Athabaska, east of the

mountains, shall pass into the new Dominion of Canada.

The population of Oregon and Washington has been temporarily depleted by the stampede for gold, following the discovery of mines in California in 1849, and Victoria has become a great outfitting post. Men are pouring into Victoria to buy goods. Presently begins the rush of gold seekers up the Fraser River. A new adventure beckons to the hardy, and cavalcades of Oregon men are driving northwards. The men of young Oregon, the men of the second generation, are seeking new goals in the wilderness, even as their fathers sought. They are traveling the old route of the northern brigades, up the bend of the Columbia, up the Okanogan, and down David Thompson's river to the Fraser. In their packs are not beaver traps but washing-pans, shovels, and picks. As they pass through the peaceful valley of the Thompson, they see Indians paddling up the river towards the fort to trade. They cast scarcely a glance at the bales in the canoes. The great quest today is not pelts but gold. A boundary line between two flags no longer holds asunder the spirit of British and American adventurers. But the romance of the fur trade is ended.

BIBLIOGRAPHICAL NOTE

FOR data on the discovery of the Northwest Coast and the Columbia River consult: Hubert Howe Bancroft's *History of the Northwest Coast*, 2 vols. (San Francisco, 1884), which includes a part of the log-book of Gray's officer, Haswell; Robert Greenhow's *History of Oregon and California* (Boston, 1847), which contains that portion of Gray's log recording his discovery of the river; W. H. Gray's *History of Oregon, 1792-1849* (Portland, 1870); T. Bulfinch's *Oregon and Eldorado* (Boston, 1866); H. S. Lyman's *History of Oregon*, 4 vols. (New York, 1903); Joseph Schafer's *History of the Pacific Northwest* (New York, 1905); E. S. Meany's *History of the State of Washington* (New York, 1909); W. R. Manning's *The Nootka Sound Controversy* in the *Annual Report* for 1904 of the American Historical Association (Washington, 1905); Arthur Kitson's *Captain James Cook, the Circumnavigator* (London, 1907); George Vancouver's *A Voyage of Discovery to the North Pacific Ocean*, 3 vols. (London, 1798); H. H. Bancroft's *Washington, Idaho, and Montana* (San Francisco, 1890); Agnes C. Laut's *Vikings of the Pacific* (New York, 1906).

For Lewis and Clark: Jefferson's *Message from the President of the United States communicating Discoveries made in Exploring the Missouri*, etc. (Washington, 1806); Olin D. Wheeler's *Trail of Lewis and Clark*, 2 vols. (New York, 1904); *The Original Journals of the Lewis and Clark Expedition*, 8 vols. (New York 1904–1905), edited by R. G. Thwaites. The last named supersedes other editions of the journals and former histories of the journey — such as those edited and revised by Elliott Coues and Biddle and Allen — by reason of its accuracy and completeness.

On the expeditions sent out by John Jacob Astor and the founding of Astoria: Washington Irving's *Astoria* (New York, 1861); Gilbert Franchère's *Narrative of a Voyage,* etc. (New York, 1854); Ross Cox's *The Columbia River, or Scenes and Adventures,* etc. 3 vols. (New York, 1832); Alexander Ross's *Adventures of the First Settlers,* etc. (London, 1849); James Parton's *Life of John Jacob Astor* (New York, 1865).

On the fur trade there is a wealth of material from which have been selected the following: H. P. Biggar's *Early Trading Companies of New France* (Toronto, 1901); Gordon Charles Davidson's *The North West Company* (Berkeley, 1918); Louis F. R. Masson's *Les Bourgeois de la Compagnie du Nord-Ouest,* 2 vols. (Quebec, 1889–1890); Agnes C. Laut's *Conquest of the Great Northwest,* 2 vols. (New York, 1909); J. Dunn's *The Oregon Territory and the British North American Fur Trade* (Philadelphia, 1845); H. M. Chittenden's *The American Fur Trade of the Far West,* 3 vols. (New York, 1902); and *History of Early Steamboat Navigation on the Missouri,* 2 vols. (New York, 1903); Elliott Coues's *New Light on the Greater North West,* containing the journals of Alexander Henry and David Thompson, 3 vols. (New York, 1897); and *Forty Years a Fur Trader* (New York, 1898); Lawrence J. Burpee's *Highways of the Fur Trade* in Royal Society of Canada *Transactions*, III, Series 3, and *The Search for the Western Sea* (London, 1908); T. C. Elliott's *Columbia Fur Trade prior to 1811* in *Washington Historical Quarterly*, vol. VI (1916); Alexander Mackenzie's *Voyages*, etc. (London, 1801); and Agnes C. Laut's transcript of Ogden's Journal in the *Quarterly* of the Oregon Historical Society, vol. XI (1910). *Hearne's Journey* edited by Joseph B. Tyrrell (1911) and *Thompson's Narrative* also edited by Tyrrell (1916) in the Champlain Society Publications, Toronto.

On Oregon during the beginnings of settlement, and missionary work: Bancroft's *History of Oregon*, 2 vols. (San Francisco, 1886–1888); W. H. Gray's *History of Oregon* (1870); F. N. Blanchet's *Historical Sketches of the Church in Oregon* (Portland, 1870); W. Barrows's *Oregon: the Struggle for Possession* (Boston, 1883) in the *American Commonwealth* series; Father de Smet's *Oregon Missions and Travels*, etc., in vol. XXIX of *Early Western Travels* (Cleveland, 1906) edited by R. G. Thwaites. Interesting material is contained in the *Quarterly* and other publications of the Oregon Historical Society and also in the publications of the Oregon Pioneer Association. For the career of McLoughlin read Bancroft's *History of Oregon* and F. V. Holman's *Dr. John McLoughlin, the Father of Oregon* (Cleveland, 1907). The latter work contains excerpts from documents, letters of McLoughlin's, and letters to him and about him by various pioneers, including Wyeth.

On the later period: Schafer's *Oregon Pioneers and American Diplomacy* in *Essays in American History* (New York, 1910); *Diary of James K. Polk*, 4 vols., edited by M. M. Quaife (Chicago, 1910); J. S. Reeves's

American Diplomacy under Tyler and Polk (1907);
Allen Johnson's *Stephen A. Douglas: a Study in American Politics* (New York, 1908); Willis Fletcher Johnson's
America's Foreign Relations, 2 vols. (New York, 1916);
Journal of the Constitutional Convention of the State of Oregon held at Salem in 1857 (Salem, 1882).

INDEX

AN OUTLINE OF THE PLAN OF THE CHRONICLES OF AMERICA

The fifty titles of the Series fall into eight topical sequences or groups, each with a dominant theme of its own—

I. *The Morning of America*
TIME: 1492-1763

THE theme of the first sequence is the struggle of nations for the possession of the New World. The mariners of four European kingdoms—Spain, Portugal, France, and England—are intent upon the discovery of a new route to Asia. They come upon the American continent which blocks the way. Spain plants colonies in the south, lured by gold. France, in pursuit of the fur trade, plants colonies in the north. Englishmen, in search of homes and of a wider freedom, occupy the Atlantic seaboard. These Englishmen come in time to need the land into which the French have penetrated by way of the St. Lawrence and the Great Lakes, and a mighty struggle between the two nations takes place in the wilderness, ending in the expulsion of the French. This sequence comprises ten volumes:

1. THE RED MAN'S CONTINENT, *by Ellsworth Huntington*
2. THE SPANISH CONQUERORS, *by Irving Berdine Richman*
3. ELIZABETHAN SEA-DOGS, *by William Wood*
4. CRUSADERS OF NEW FRANCE, *by William Bennett Munro*
5. PIONEERS OF THE OLD SOUTH, *by Mary Johnston*
6. THE FATHERS OF NEW ENGLAND, *by Charles M. Andrews*
7. DUTCH AND ENGLISH ON THE HUDSON, *by Maud Wilder Goodwin*
8. THE QUAKER COLONIES, *by Sydney G. Fisher*
9. COLONIAL FOLKWAYS, *by Charles M. Andrews*
10. THE CONQUEST OF NEW FRANCE, *by George M. Wrong*

II. *The Winning of Independence*
TIME: 1763-1815

The French peril has passed, and the great territory between the Alleghanies and the Mississippi is now open to the Englishmen on the seaboard with no enemy to contest their right of way except the Indian. But the question arises whether these Englishmen in the New World shall submit to political dictation from the King and Parliament of England. To decide this question the War of the Revolution is fought; the Union is born and the second war with England follows. Seven volumes:

11. THE EVE OF THE REVOLUTION, *by Carl Becker*
12. WASHINGTON AND HIS COMRADES IN ARMS, *by George M. Wrong*
13. THE FATHERS OF THE CONSTITUTION, *by Max Farrand*
14. WASHINGTON AND HIS COLLEAGUES, *by Henry Jones Ford*
15. JEFFERSON AND HIS COLLEAGUES, *by Allen Johnson*
16. JOHN MARSHALL AND THE CONSTITUTION, *by Edward S. Corwin*
17. THE FIGHT FOR A FREE SEA, *by Ralph D. Paine*

III. *The Vision of the West*
TIME: 1750-1890

The theme of the third sequence is the American frontier—the conquest of the continent from the Alleghanies to the Pacific Ocean. The story covers nearly a century and a half, from the first crossing of the Alleghanies by the backwoodsmen of Pennsylvania, Virginia, and the Carolinas (about 1750) to the heyday of the cowboy on the Great Plains in the latter part of the nineteenth century. This is the marvelous tale of the greatest migrations in history, told in nine volumes as follows:

18. PIONEERS OF THE OLD SOUTHWEST, *by Constance Lindsay Skinner*
19. THE OLD NORTHWEST, *by Frederic Austin Ogg*
20. THE REIGN OF ANDREW JACKSON, *by Frederic Austin Ogg*
21. THE PATHS OF INLAND COMMERCE, *by Archer B. Hulbert*
22. ADVENTURERS OF OREGON, *by Constance Lindsay Skinner*
23. THE SPANISH BORDERLANDS, *by Herbert E. Bolton*
24. TEXAS AND THE MEXICAN WAR, *by Nathaniel W. Stephenson*
25. THE FORTY-NINERS, *by Stewart Edward White*
26. THE PASSING OF THE FRONTIER, *by Emerson Hough*

IV. *The Storm of Secession*

TIME: 1830-1876

The curtain rises on the gathering storm of secession. The theme of the fourth sequence is the preservation of the Union, which carries with it the extermination of slavery. Six volumes as follows:

V. *The Intellectual Life*

Two volumes follow on the higher national life, telling of the nation's great teachers and interpreters:

VI. *The Epic of Commerce and Industry*

The sixth sequence is devoted to the romance of industry and business, and the dominant theme is the transformation caused by the inflow of immigrants and the development and utilization of mechanics on a great scale. The long age of muscular power has passed, and the era of mechanical power has brought with it a new kind of civilization. Eight volumes:

VII. *The Era of World Power*

The seventh sequence carries on the story of government and diplomacy and political expansion from the Reconstruction (1876) to the present day, in six volumes:

VIII. *Our Neighbors*

Now to round out the story of the continent, the Hispanic peoples on the south and the Canadians on the north are taken up where they were dropped further back in the Series, and these peoples are followed down to the present day:

The Chronicles of America is thus a great synthesis, giving a new projection and a new interpretation of American History. These narratives are works of real scholarship, for every one is written after an exhaustive examination of the sources. Many of them contain new facts; some of them —such as those by Howland, Seymour, and Hough—are founded on intimate personal knowledge. But the originality of the Series lies, not chiefly in new facts, but rather in new ideas and new combinations of old facts.

The General Editor of the Series is Dr. Allen Johnson, Chairman of the Department of History of Yale University, and the entire work has been planned, prepared, and published under the control of the Council's Committee on Publications of Yale University.

YALE UNIVERSITY PRESS

143 ELM STREET, NEW HAVEN
522 FIFTH AVENUE, NEW YORK

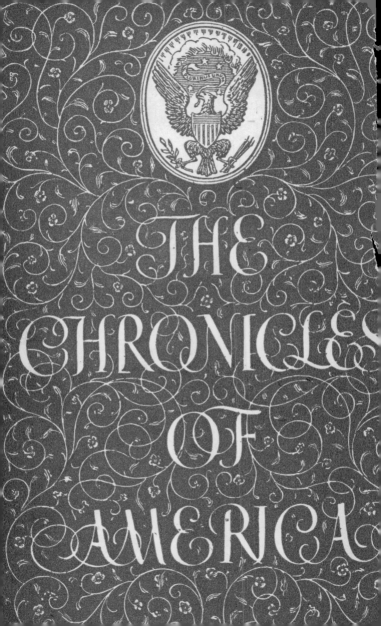

THE
CHRONICLES
OF
AMERICA